FORMED IN CHRI

C000231185

ABOUT THE SER

Who is Jesus Christ? What does it mean to kno ... ... Church and her sacraments have to do with him? How are we to follow him?

These are the questions at the heart of the Catholic faith, and these are the questions the Formed in Christ series answers. Rooted in the story of Salvation History and steeped in the writings of the Fathers and Doctors of the Church, this series of high school textbooks from the St. Paul Center seeks to engage minds and hearts as it presents the tenets of the Catholic faith in Scripture and Tradition.

Over the course of this comprehensive, four-year curriculum, students will learn the fundamentals of Church teaching on the Person and mission of Jesus Christ, Sacred Scripture, the Church, the sacraments, morality, Church history, vocations, Catholic social teaching, and more. Just as important, they'll be invited, again and again, to enter more deeply into a relationship with Christ, growing in love of him as they grow in knowledge of him.

PUBLISHED

Evidence of Things Unseen: An Introduction to Fundamental Theology
Andrew Willard Jones and Louis St. Hilaire.
Edited by Stimpson Chapman

The Word Became Flesh: An Introduction to Christology
Andrew Willard Jones. Edited by Emily Stimpson Chapman

That You Might Have Life: An Introduction to the Paschal Mystery of Christ
Louis St. Hilaire. Edited by Emily Stimpson Chapman

I Will Build My Church: An Introduction to Ecclesiology
Andrew Willard Jones. Edited by Emily Stimpson Chapman

Do This in Remembrance: An Introduction to the Sacraments
Jacob Wood. Edited by Emily Stimpson Chapman

Christ Alive in Us: An Introduction to Moral Theology
John Meinert and Emily Stimpson Chapman

DO THIS IN REMEMBRANCE

AN INTRODUCTION TO THE SACRAMENTS

DO THIS IN REMEMBRANCE

An Introduction to the Sacraments

JACOB W. WOOD
Edited by Emily Stimpson Chapman

EMMAUS
ROAD
PUBLISHING

www.emmausroad.org
Steubenville, Ohio

In Grateful Recognition of Lawrence Joseph & Lynn Marie Blanford

Emmaus Road Publishing
1468 Parkview Circle
Steubenville, Ohio 43952

Library of Congress Control Number: 2019934892

ISBN 978-1-949013-47-4

Cover image: *The Last Supper* (c. 1562), Juan de Juanes, Museo del Prado, Madrid, Spain

Cover design and layout by Margaret Ryland

TABLE OF CONTENTS

Abbreviations

ANF: *The Ante-Nicene Fathers: Translations of the Writings of the Fathers Down to A.D. 325.* Edited by Alexander Roberts, James Donaldson, and A. Cleveland Coxe. 10 Vols. Buffalo: The Christian Literature Publishing Company, 1885–96.

CCC: *The Catechism of the Catholic Church.* Second Edition. Vatican City: Libreria Editrice Vaticana, 2000.

CIC: The 1983 Code of Canon Law, Latin-English Edition. New English Translation, Second Printing. Canon Law Society of America, 2012.

CSEL: *Corpus Scriptorum Ecclesiasticorum Latinorum.* 101 Vols. Vienna: Österreichische Akademie der Wissenschaften, 1869–Present.

DH: *Enchiridion symbolorum definitionum et declarationum de rebus fidei et morum.* Edited by Heinrich Denzinger and Peter Hünnermann. Translated by Robert Fastiggi and Anne Englund Nash. 43rd edition. San Francisco: Ignatius Press, 2012.

Leonine: Thomas Aquinas. *Opera Omnia.* 50 vols. Rome/Paris: Commissio Leonina, 1882–Present.

NPNF: *A Select Library of the Nicene and Post-Nicene Fathers of the Christian Church.* Edited by Philip Schaff and Henry Wace. 14 Vols. New York: The Christian Literature Publishing Company, 1890–1900.

Part I

THE SACRAMENTAL ECONOMY

ASSIGNED READING
Genesis 1–2
John 11
CCC 1066–1209

All throughout the day we are surrounded by words. We talk with friends at school, we write text messages to friends elsewhere, we listen to the radio in the car, we watch television at home, we read books at night. Words help us share our thoughts, feelings, and desires with others; they help us understand the thoughts, feelings, and desires of others as well. Scientists estimate that the average person speaks about ten to fifteen thousand words per day. That's enough to fill fifty books per year!

Without words, we would be altogether isolated from others. In fact, we would even be isolated from ourselves. Our very thoughts require words. Sure, we can picture things in our minds without words, like trees, but the moment that we want to think about what we see in our mind's eye we have to form an idea, which is a collection of words: "This is a tree."

The purpose of a word is to point to something. When we think, our ideas point us to the things we are thinking about. When we speak, our spoken words point others to our ideas. When we write, our written words point others to what we would have said if we were present with them. In this way, our whole relationship to the world, to other people, and to ourselves is characterized by words.

Because God made us, he knows how much we depend on words (CCC 1146); and so, since he wanted to enter into a relationship with us, he decided to use words at every step of the way. In the beginning, God created all that exists with the words "Let there be" (Gen 1:3). When God wanted to draw the people of Israel into a relationship with himself, he gave them the Decalogue, which is another way of saying "Ten Words" (Exod 20). Finally, when the fullness of time had come, God sent his own Word, Jesus, to live, die, and rise again among us. We call Jesus the "Word of God" (John 1:1) because he does for God what words do for us: he shows us who God is and what God has in mind for us.

There's a big difference, though, between our words and God's words. Our words indicate our thoughts, but our thoughts don't make anything happen. We can think for hours about doing our homework, but if we don't act on our words, the homework never gets done. On a more serious level, we can have important conversations about how we would like to solve world hunger, but if we don't go down to a soup kitchen, nobody actually gets fed. Since our words don't make things happen, we can even say one thing and do another: we can lie, cheat, and deceive. In technical language, we say that our words are *signs* (they point to things), but they are not *causes* (they don't make things happen).

It's not the same with God. God can never lie, cheat, or deceive because there is no gap between his words and his actions. All God has to do is talk about doing homework and it gets done, because everything that God says, happens. God's words are both signs *and* causes; and since Jesus is God, Jesus' words are signs and causes too. When Jesus said to the storm, "Be still!" (Mark 4:39), his words made the storm stop. When he said to the paralytic, "Rise, take up your bed and go home" (Matt 9:6; Mark 2:11; Luke 5:24), his words made the man's legs better. When Jesus said to Lazarus who had been dead for four days, "Laz'arus, come out" (John 11:43), his words made Lazarus get up and walk out of the tomb.

Importantly, Jesus did not keep the power to speak God's words to himself. St. Paul tells us this when he writes that Jesus never thought of his equality with God as something to be kept to himself (Phil 2:6). On the contrary, he gave the Catholic Church the power to use his words in seven ways. Those seven ways are the seven sacraments: Baptism, Confirmation, Eucharist, Penance and Reconciliation, Anointing of the Sick, Holy Orders, and Marriage. In each of the seven sacraments, a minister of the Church speaks the words of Jesus and does something. Since the minister's actions are empowered by Jesus' words, things happen—just like on the day of creation and on the day when Jesus raised Lazarus from the dead.

Chapter 1

DEFINITION OF SACRAMENT

The word "sacrament" comes from a Latin word, *sacramentum*. In ancient Rome, *sacramentum* was a legal term. It referred to a bond you posted at the beginning of a lawsuit as the proof of your good faith that you would pay the judgment if you lost. By extension it also referred to the oath you took at the beginning of military service, which is itself a pledge of good faith. But for the Romans, taking an oath to enter military service was not just a pledge of good faith; it was also a religious commitment. By the time of Caesar Augustus, many Romans thought that the Roman emperor was a god, and the worship of the emperor became an official part of Roman life. When a man entered the emperor's service, the Romans considered it a permanent religious commitment, and the man received a branding with a hot iron as a permanent mark of that commitment.[1]

The early Church writer Tertullian seems to have been the first person to sense the similarity between the words that Jesus gave to the Church and the words professed by Roman soldiers upon entering the emperor's service. Not that there is any similarity between God and the Roman emperor—the imperial cult was idolatrous!—but both sets of practices involve the profession of words that began a person's entrance

---

[1] In the Eastern part of the Roman Empire, where people spoke Greek instead of Latin, they used the Greek word *mysterion* instead of the Latin word *sacramentum*. Although *mysterion* does not have the same association with lawsuits or oaths, it captured the inner reality referred to by the outward actions (CCC 774).

to a new community and a new way of life.[2]

At the same time, however great the similarities between God's words and the Roman military oath may have been, Tertullian was very careful to emphasize the differences. He thought that the kind of service to the emperor required by the Roman *sacramentum* was absolutely incompatible with the service that Christians owe to God alone,[3] and that even though other religions have their own rites involving life-changing words and commitments to new forms of life, none of them possess the truly transformative power of the words that God speaks in the sacraments of the Catholic Church.[4]

It was St. Augustine who best articulated the difference between the sacraments of the Church and the customs of Roman soldiers.[5] The transformative power behind the sacraments of the Catholic Church, he observes, is the Holy Spirit—the same Holy Spirit who hovered over the waters at creation when God spoke the words of creation (Gen 1:2), overshadowed Mary when the Word of God was Incarnate in her womb (Luke 1:35), who is "poured into our hearts" when we are united to friendship and fellowship with God (Rom 5:5), and who bestows upon those who are united in friendship and fellowship with God "the unity of the Spirit in the bond of peace" (Eph 4:3). Only those who belong to that unity—outwardly or by desire—receive the Holy Spirit, because Jesus entrusted that Spirit to his Church.[6] Even though the sacraments of the Church have certain similarities to secular rites of passage and the ceremonies of other religions, no other words give us the Holy Spirit like those of the seven sacraments.

St. Augustine was also one of the first Church Fathers to articulate very clearly why the Holy Spirit makes such a difference. It is because the Holy Spirit gives us *grace*. According to the Catechism of the Catholic Church, "Grace is *favor*, the free and undeserved help that God gives us to respond to his call to become children of God, adoptive sons, partak-

---

2   Tertullian, *Adversus Marcionem* 4.34.
3   Tertullian, *De corona militis* 11.
4   Tertullian, *De praescriptione haereticorum* 40.
5   Augustine, *De baptismo* 3.16.21.
6   Augustine, *De baptismo* 1.2.3; John 16:13; 20:22; Acts 1:8; CCC 846–848.

ers of the divine nature and of eternal life [Cf. *Jn* 1:12–18; 17:3; *Rom* 8:14–17; *2 Pet* 1:3–4]" (CCC 1996). In giving us his grace, God helps us to come closer to him in two ways.

Sometimes he intervenes in our lives in a special, more immediate way—like when we sin and he wants to call us back to himself, or when he wants us to take a big step in the spiritual life like embracing a vocation to religious life, the priesthood, or marriage. In those situations, we say that God gives us "actual grace," because the grace he gives us makes us act. Other times, after we have acted on the graces that God has given us, he intervenes in our lives in a stable, more permanent way—like when he strengthens us in faith after Baptism, or in love after marriage. In those situations we say that God gives us "habitual grace," because he causes a habit in us—a stable disposition.[7]

The greatest of all habits we call "sanctifying grace." "Sanctifying grace is an habitual gift, a stable and supernatural disposition that perfects the soul itself to enable it to live with God, to act by his love" (CCC 2000). The goal of sanctifying grace is the complete transformation of our souls so that we may "become partakers of the divine nature" (2 Pet 1:4; CCC 1129).

We are now ready for a definition of a sacrament: "The sacraments are efficacious signs of grace, instituted by Christ and entrusted to the Church, by which divine life is dispensed to us" (CCC 1131). Although the definition may seem complicated, you already know everything you need to be able to break it down and understand it:

"The sacraments . . ." Sacraments are the transformative words of God that he gave to human persons to speak.

". . . are efficacious signs . . ." They are *signs* because each of the seven sacraments points to something that God wants to do in us; they are *efficacious* signs because, like all of God's words, they also make that thing happen.

". . . of grace . . ." Grace is the means by which God brings about in us what he wants to in the sacraments; it is the effect in us caused by the Holy Spirit's presence.

---

[7] Thomas Aquinas, *Summa Theologiae* (hereafter cited at ST) Ia–IIae, q. 49, a. 1.

"... **instituted by Christ...**" The sacraments are given to us by Jesus, the Word of God.

"... **and entrusted to the Church...**" The sacraments are entrusted to the Church because the Holy Spirit, whom they give us, is entrusted to the Church.

"... **by which divine life is dispensed to us.**" The principal grace that the Holy Spirit gives us through the sacraments is sanctifying grace, which brings us into friendship and fellowship with God now, and prepares us to dwell with him in glory hereafter.

The Church and the Sacramental Economy of Salvation

Although the seven sacraments of the Church are the only sacraments properly speaking, the Church uses the word "sacrament" analogously for things that act like sacraments, because they point to something and make it happen. For example, Jesus says that "He who has seen me has seen the Father" (John 14:9), and St. John tells us that when we have faith in God, Jesus makes the Father present in us (1 John 2:24; 2 John 9). As the Word of God, Jesus points us to the Father and makes the Father present to us. We can therefore call Jesus a sacrament of God (see CCC 1088–1090).

The same is true of the Church. The Church is not a sacrament properly speaking. At the same time, it points to the fulfillment of the Greatest Commandments—the love of God and the love of neighbor—and makes us able to fulfill them (Matt 22:35–40). The Acts of the Apostles tells us that from its earliest days, the Church was a sign to the world of our union with God and with one another (Acts 4:32–33). What is more, that spiritual union stuck out as something important to nonbelievers. Tertullian tells us that in the early days of Christianity outsiders would marvel at the love of God in the Church:

> See, [the pagans] say, how [Christians] love one another ... how they are ready even to die for one another. ... And [the pagans]

are angry with us [Christians], too, because we call each other brethren; for no other reason, as I think, than because among themselves names of consanguinity are assumed in mere pretense of affection. But we are your brethren as well, by the law of our common mother nature, though you are hardly men, because brothers so unkind. At the same time, how much more fittingly they are called and counted brothers who have been led to the knowledge of God as their common Father, who have drunk in one spirit of holiness, who from the same womb of a common ignorance have agonized into the same light of truth![8]

Because the Church not only *points* to the fulfillment of the Greatest Commandments but, by giving us the sacraments, actually makes us able to *fulfill* them (CCC 1123), the Church can be called a "universal sacrament of salvation" (CCC 776): something that points to salvation, and makes it happen. Just like in Tertullian's day, it's something that gets people's attention!

QUESTIONS FOR REVIEW

1. What was the meaning of the word *sacramentum* in the ancient Roman world?
2. What is the difference between the sacraments of the Church and the customs of Roman soldiers?
3. What is sanctifying grace?
4. How does the Church define "sacrament"?
5. Why do we call the Church "the universal sacrament of salvation"?

QUESTIONS FOR DISCUSSION

6. How important are the sacraments in your life right now? What are you looking forward to learning about the sacraments as you study them with the aid of this book?

---

[8] Tertullian, *Apologeticum* 39 (ANF 3:46).

7. Have you ever felt particularly close to God after receiving a sacrament? If so, describe your experience. If not, or if you have not yet received any sacraments, have you ever known anyone who did feel this way?

Chapter 2

REDEMPTION IS MEDIATED
THROUGH THE SACRAMENTS

When we call the Church a "universal sacrament of salvation," it's tempting to think that the Church possesses some sort of magic power by
which it dispenses salvation and that the sacraments are like potions we
take from the Church to cure our spiritual ills. Nothing, however, could
be further from the truth. Just like an individual Christian depends
entirely on God's grace to make progress in the spiritual life, so too does
the Church depend entirely on God's power to give us the sacraments.
Remember, human words are *signs* but not *causes*; there's a gap between
what we say and what we do. Only God's words make things happen just
because he says them. If the sacraments were merely the Church's words,
they could point to what God was thinking about but they could never
make it happen; the sacraments only give us the Holy Spirit because they
are backed by God's words (CCC 1084).

How can the Church speak God's words? Imagine, for a moment,
that you want to hammer a nail into a piece of wood. You line up the
nail, pick up your hammer, and—*whack!*—the nail goes into the wood.
Let me ask you a question. Who or what hammered the nail? Did you
hammer the nail or did the hammer do it? It's tricky. On the one hand,
the hammer is the thing that struck the nail—if you struck the nail with
just your hand, you'd be in for a trip to the emergency room. On the other

hand, hammers generally don't go around striking nails unless someone picks them up, do they?

As it turns out, it's not just a tricky question; it's a trick question. The answer is that you both did it because you hammered the nail by means *of* the hammer. In technical terms, we say that the hammer is your instrument—not as though it were a flute, a guitar, or a saxophone (that's a different kind of instrument), but because the hammer is your tool. Since you're the one who picks up the hammer, we call you the *primary cause* of the nail going into the wood; since the hammer is your tool, we call it your *instrumental cause.*[1]

The sacraments work in a similar way. Jesus has a goal in mind: he wants to put sanctifying grace in our souls to bring us into friendship with him. But he does not want to force his grace into us. Trying to force someone into a relationship is like trying to force a nail with just your hand—it's a bad idea, and someone's going to get hurt. Instead, Jesus wants to offer us his Holy Spirit in such a way that we would want to accept it (CCC 2022). So, like an expert craftsman (Jesus was the son of a carpenter, wasn't he?), Jesus picks the right tools for the job. Instead of sending grace like thunderbolts from on high and forcing us to receive it, he comes to us gently in familiar people, the ministers of the Church, performing familiar activities, like washing and eating, and speaking words that we can understand. He does this so that we can freely accept the graces he wants to give us and comfortably cooperate with the people he asks to distribute his grace (CCC 1148).

Convincing us to want grace took time. So, instead of giving us the sacraments all at once, God prepared us for a sacramental relationship with him through a series of covenants in the Old Testament. Each covenant included some sign or symbol that pointed out what God was doing in that covenant and prepared us to receive the sacraments that Jesus was going to establish.

Through Noah, God made a covenant with all creation not to destroy it by flood again; God pointed out his intention by giving us rainbows, a sign of peace after storms (Gen 9:12–17). With Abraham,

---

[1] Aquinas, ST IIIa, q. 64, a. 1.

God made a series of covenants in which he promised to give land and children to Abraham, and blessings to Abraham, his children, and all the world through them (Gen 12:1–3); God pointed out what he was doing by asking Abraham to undergo circumcision, a sign of his family's total dependence on God for all those blessings, especially children (Gen 17:9–14). Through Moses, God made a covenant in which he formed Abraham's family into a free nation (Exod 24:1–8); God pointed out what he was doing by asking the nation of Israel to keep the Passover, a sign of the loving care and protection by which he brought them out of slavery into the Promised Land (Exod 12:27). To David, God promised an everlasting line of kings to rule God's people (2 Sam 7:4–17); God pointed out what he was doing by having David and his successors anointed with an oil symbolizing permanent consecration to God (Exod 30:30–33; 2 Sam 2:1–7).

The signs in the Old Testament were not sacraments properly speaking. Although they were actions that God asked the people to perform, God did not give the people his own words to accompany the actions, and so the actions did not make things happen in the same way that sacraments do. Circumcision was a sign of Abraham's total dependence on God for his family, but it was possible to get circumcised on the outside without acknowledging your total inward dependence on God, because there was nothing about circumcision that *made* you put your trust in God (Rom 2:25–29). The Passover sacrifice was a sign of the nation of Israel's total dependence on God for their freedom, but it was possible to participate in the sacrifice without any regard for one's own or others' freedom in God, because there was nothing about the Passover sacrifice that *made* a person thankful for freedom (Isa 1:10–23). The royal anointing was a sign of the Davidic dynasty's total dependence on God for its authority, but it was possible for David and his successors to receive an anointing without paying any attention to God at all, because there was nothing about the anointing that *made* them obedient to God (2 Kings 21:1–18).

Much to the contrary, St. Paul tells us that although the signs that people performed in the Old Testament prefigured the sacraments of the Catholic Church, part of the point of those signs was that their powerlessness to make us trusting, thankful, and obedient would prepare us to accept the sacraments of the Catholic Church as the means by which God would actually cause those virtues in us (Rom 7:7–25; Heb 7:11–28).

The Old Testament signs passed away when Jesus came. As we saw above, since Jesus is God, things happen when he speaks: calming a storm, healing a paralytic, raising a man from the dead. Those are all physical things that Jesus did with his words. But Jesus also did spiritual things with his words. Just as surely as the storm calmed when he said, "Be still!" the demon left when Jesus said, "come out . . . !" (Luke 4:35). Just as surely as the paralytic moved when Jesus said, "Rise," the paralytic was made a friend of God when Jesus said, "your sins are forgiven" (Mark 2:5). Just as surely as Lazarus rose from physical death when Jesus said, "come out," so also the sinful woman rose from spiritual death when Jesus spoke to her the same words of pardon he spoke to the paralyzed man (Luke 7:48).

The most powerful words that Jesus ever spoke were those he uttered while hanging on the Cross (CCC 2605). Among the last of those were the words "It is finished" (John 19:30). With these words, Jesus not only pointed out that he had completed the work of our salvation, but that he completed the work that God had been preparing us to accept since he made the first covenant with us (CCC 601). By *giving up* his spirit, Jesus *gave us* his Spirit (CCC 713). It is the Holy Spirit who gives us grace through the sacraments and so unites the members of the Catholic Church into fellowship with God and with one another.

When Jesus rose from the dead, he breathed his Holy Spirit on the Apostles in a particular way so that they could give that Holy Spirit to others (John 20:22). St. Jerome explains the significance of this event:

> Therefore on the first day of the Resurrection, when the Lord says, "whose sins you forgive are forgiven them; whose sins you retain are retained," they received the grace of the Holy Spirit to forgive sins, to baptize, to make children of God, and to bestow the spirit of adoption upon believers.[2]

---

[2] Jerome, Epistle 120.9 (CSEL 55:494).

But just as Jesus did not keep the power to speak God's words to himself so also he commanded the Apostles not to keep the gift of the Holy Spirit to themselves:

And Jesus came and said to them, "All authority in heaven and on earth has been given to me. Go therefore and make disciples of all nations, baptizing them in the name of the Father and of the Son and of the Holy Spirit, teaching them to observe all that I have commanded you; and behold, I am with you always, to the close of the age." (Matt 28:18–20)

The Apostles were faithful to this charge. From that day forward they went out into the world, bringing the Holy Spirit that they had received from Jesus to others through the sacraments (CCC 2). Their mission and their action continues in the Church even to the present day. Thus the Church has continued since the day of Pentecost as a universal sacrament of salvation: pointing people to the love of God and to the love of neighbor by her life and uniting them in that love through the seven sacraments.

Although God's purpose for all of the seven sacraments is in one sense the same, different sacraments have different ways in which they give us grace and prepare us for glory. That being the case, the Church usually groups the sacraments into three categories based upon how they give us grace and prepare us for glory (CCC 1210–1211). Those that first bring us into fellowship and friendship with God we call the "Sacraments of Initiation." Those that fix the problems in our fellowship and friendship with God we call the "Sacraments of Healing." Those that help us help others in their fellowship and friendship with God we call the "Sacraments at the Service of Communion." The Sacraments of Initiation are Baptism, Confirmation, and Eucharist. The Sacraments of Healing are Reconciliation and Anointing of the Sick. The Sacraments at the Service of Communion are Holy Orders and Marriage. We will discuss each of these categories in turn, beginning with the Sacraments of Initiation. For each sacrament, we will cover the following:

- how God prepared his people for the sacrament with signs in the Old Testament and instituted it in the New Testament;
- how, by whom, and for whom the sacrament is celebrated;
- what the sacrament's effects are; and
- how to live out the sacrament.

SELECTED READING
The Catechism of the Catholic Church, nos. 770–776

The Church is in history, but at the same time she transcends it. It is only "with the eyes of faith" [*Roman Catechism* I, 10, 20] that one can see her in her visible reality and at the same time in her spiritual reality as bearer of divine life.

The Church - both visible and spiritual
"The one mediator, Christ, established and ever sustains here on earth his holy Church, the community of faith, hope, and charity, as a visible organization through which he communicates truth and grace to all men" [*LG* 8 §1]. The Church is at the same time:

- a "society structured with hierarchical organs and the mystical body of Christ;
- the visible society and the spiritual community;
- the earthly Church and the Church endowed with heavenly riches" [*LG* 8].

These dimensions together constitute "one complex reality which comes together from a human and a divine element" [*LG* 8]:

The Church is essentially both human and divine, visible but endowed with invisible realities, zealous in action and dedicated to contemplation, present in the world, but as a pilgrim, so constituted that in her the human is directed toward and subordinated to the divine, the visible to the invisible, action to contemplation, and this present world to that city yet to come, the object of our quest [*SC* 2; cf. *Heb* 13:14].

O humility! O sublimity! Both tabernacle of cedar and sanctuary of God; earthly dwelling and celestial palace; house of clay and royal hall; body of death and temple of light; and at last both object of scorn to the proud and bride of Christ! She is black but beautiful, O daughters of Jerusalem, for even if the labor and pain of her long exile may have discolored her, yet heaven's beauty has adorned her [St. Bernard of Clairvaux, *In Cant. Sermo* 27: 14: PL 183: 920D].

The Church - mystery of men's union with God

It is in the Church that Christ fulfills and reveals his own mystery as the purpose of God's plan: "to unite all things in him" [*Eph* 1:10]. St. Paul calls the nuptial union of Christ and the Church "a great mystery." Because she is united to Christ as to her bridegroom, she becomes a mystery in her turn [*Eph* 5:32; 3:9-11; 5:25-27]. Contemplating this mystery in her, Paul exclaims: "Christ in you, the hope of glory" [*Col* 1:27].

In the Church this communion of men with God, in the "love [that] never ends," is the purpose which governs everything in her that is a sacramental means, tied to this passing world [*1 Cor* 13:8; cf. *LG* 48]. "[The Church's] structure is totally ordered to the holiness of Christ's members. And holiness is measured according to the 'great mystery' in which the Bride responds with the gift of love to the gift of the Bridegroom" [John Paul II, *MD* 27]. Mary goes before us all in the holiness that is the Church's mystery as "the bride without spot or wrinkle" [*Eph* 5:27]. This is why the "Marian" dimension of the Church precedes the "Petrine" [Cf. John Paul II, *MD* 27].

The universal Sacrament of Salvation

The Greek word *mysterion* was translated into Latin by two terms: *mysterium* and *sacramentum*. In later usage the term *sacramentum* emphasizes the visible sign of the hidden reality of salvation which was indicated by the term *mysterium*. In this sense, Christ himself is the mystery of salvation: "For there is no other mystery of God, except Christ" [St. Augustine, *Ep.* 187, 11, 34: PL 33, 846]. The saving work of his holy and sanctifying humanity is the sacrament of salvation, which is revealed and active in the Church's sacraments (which the Eastern Churches also call "the holy mysteries"). The seven sacraments are the signs and instruments by which the Holy Spirit spreads the grace of Christ the head throughout the Church which is his Body. The Church, then, both contains and communicates the invisible grace she signifies. It is in this analogical sense, that the Church is called a "sacrament."

"The Church, in Christ, is like a sacrament—a sign and instrument, that is, of communion with God and of unity among all men" [*LG* 1]. The Church's first purpose is to be the sacrament of the inner union of men with God. Because men's communion with one another is rooted in that union with God, the Church is also the sacrament of the unity of the human race. In her, this unity is already begun, since she gathers men "from every nation, from all tribes and peoples and tongues" [*Rev* 7:9]; at the same time, the Church is the "sign and instrument" of the full realization of the unity yet to come.

As sacrament, the Church is Christ's instrument. "She is taken up by him also as the instrument for the salvation of all," "the universal sacrament of salvation," by which Christ is "at once manifesting and actualizing the mystery of God's love for men" [*LG* 9 §2, 48 §2; *GS* 45 §1]. The Church "is the visible plan of God's love for humanity," because God desires "that the whole human race may become one People of God, form one Body of Christ, and be built up into one temple of the Holy Spirit" [Paul VI, June 22, 1973; *AG* 7 §2; cf. *LG* 17].

QUESTIONS FOR REVIEW

1. What is the difference between a primary cause and an instrumental cause?
2. How did God prepare humanity for a sacramental relationship with himself in the Old Testament?
3. What is the difference between the covenantal signs in the Old Testament and the sacraments of the New Testament?
4. What happened to the Old Testament signs when Jesus came?
5. Into what three categories does the Church typically divide the sacraments?

QUESTIONS FOR DISCUSSION

1. Has there ever been a time when God worked through you to do good to another? Describe what that felt like.
2. Oftentimes we have to wait for God's best gifts in our lives. Can you think of a time when you had to wait to receive something good? How did God prepare your heart to receive it while you were waiting?

Part II

BAPTISM

Every year, adult converts receive the Sacraments of Initiation all at once on Easter Vigil. First they receive Baptism, then Confirmation, then Eucharist. That is the original order of those sacraments (Acts 8:14–17, 19:1–7), which has been observed in the Church since time immemorial.[1] There is a certain logic to this order. First you are brought into a relationship with God through Jesus in Baptism, then you are empowered in that relationship by the Spirit of Jesus in Confirmation, then you reach the summit of that relationship in union with Jesus in the Eucharist. But this is not the order in which most Catholic children in the Latin Rite receive those sacraments today. Why the difference?

Generally speaking, since the Church wants you to be in friendship and fellowship with God, she offers you each sacrament as soon as you are ready to make profitable use of the graces that God offers to you through it. Adults are already prepared to make profitable use of the graces of each sacrament, so when an adult becomes Catholic, the Church gives them all the Sacraments of Initiation in the original order. Children, however, reach appropriate ages for different sacraments at different times. Each and every infant needs the salvation that Baptism offers (CCC 1250); each and every person who is old enough to recognize the presence of Jesus in the Eucharist needs to be united with him there (see John 6:53; 1 Cor 11:29); each and every person who is ready to take on the responsibilities of mature Christian witness needs to be confirmed in the Holy Spirit to do so (Acts 8:17).

Infants aren't old enough to discern the body of Jesus in the Eucharist, nor are small children always ready to assume the responsibilities of

---

[1]   See Cyril of Jerusalem, *Mystagogical Catecheses* 2–4.

mature Christian witness. So in the Latin Rite, the Church waits to give us each sacrament until we are ready for it: Baptism when we are born, Eucharist when we reach the age of reason at about seven years old, and Confirmation when we are ready for the responsibilities of mature Christian witness. Even if it is not absolutely necessary to do things in this way (in the Eastern Rites of the Catholic Church even infants receive Confirmation and Eucharist), the better we are able to prepare ourselves for the celebration of each sacrament, the better we are able to profit from the graces offered to us therein.[2]

In what follows, we are going to assume the original order of the Sacraments of Initiation. Everything that will be said applies to you, whenever you may have received or may receive these sacraments.

Baptism is the first of the seven sacraments, as well as the first Sacrament of Initiation. Its name comes from the Greek word *baptizein*, which means to "dip, plunge, drench," or "be soaked" (see CCC 1214). In the most basic form of Baptism, a parish priest says to the person who is going to be baptized, "I baptize you in the name of the Father, and of the Son, and of the Holy Spirit," and immerses the person in water each time one of the Persons of the Trinity is mentioned (CCC 1239–1240).[3] In lieu of a complete immersion, water can be poured over the head, as is customary throughout the Latin Rite; this is called "baptism by infusion" (CCC 1239; CIC, Canon 854). "Through baptism men and women are freed from sin, are reborn as children of God, and, configured to Christ by an indelible character, are incorporated into the Church" (CIC, Canon 849).

---

[2] See Aquinas, ST supplement, q. 6, a. 5.
[3] Code of Canon Law (hereafter cited in text as CIC), Canon 530, §1. In the East, the passive voice is used, but the meaning of the words is the same. "The servant of God, N., is baptized in the name of the Father, and of the Son, and of the Holy Spirit."

Chapter 1

Understanding the
Sacrament

Old Testament

Assigned Reading
Genesis 6–9
Exodus 14–15

God created the heavens and the earth out of nothing (CCC 296), but when God set about the work of creation, water was one of the first things he made. Even before God said, "Let there be light" on the first day, he had already made water and his Spirit was hovering over it (Gen 1:2). On the second and third days, when God created the seas and the clouds, he did not create more water; he simply separated the water he had already made into waters below (the seas) and waters above (the clouds), arranging things so that dry land would appear from the waters below and adequate rain would come forth from the waters above to produce edible crops (Gen 1:7, 9–13).

On the sixth day, when God made Adam and Eve to dwell in friendship and fellowship with him in Paradise, our first parents could see in their relationship with water a sign of their relationship with God. Just as they depended on water to sustain their lives, both by drinking the waters below and by eating the crops watered by the waters above, so also they depended for their whole sustenance on God, who gave them those waters, who kept the waters below at bay and who kept the waters above fruitful (see Acts 14:17).

When Adam and Eve sinned against God, they could still see a sign of their relationship with God in their relationship with water; only now it was a sign of brokenness. Whereas previously the waters below gave Adam and Eve life by drinking, now sometimes Adam and Eve had to suffer from too little water (thirst) or too much (drowning); whereas previously the waters above gave them food by nourishing their crops, now sometimes they had to suffer from too little rain (which caused famine) or too much (which caused flood). There was a purpose to this imbalance. Just as God taught the Israelites about their need for him through the ineffectiveness of the signs of the Old Testament to make them trusting, thankful, and obedient, so also he taught all of humanity about their need for him through the inability of the natural world to sustain them in a trouble-free life.

Because God is Provident, he never allows any evil to occur without bringing forth some greater good (CCC 311). The *first* example of this is the *Protoevangelium* (or "first gospel"), the promise of a savior that occurs immediately after the first sin (Gen 3:15; CCC 410). The *best* example of this is the Cross, in which God turned the worst of all possible evils, deicide (which means to kill God), into the best of all possible goods, salvation (CCC 312). But between the first and best examples of God's Providence, there were numerous other examples, especially those connected with the gradual restoration of humanity to friendship and fellowship with God through a series of covenants.

Throughout the covenants in the Old Testament, God took the evil effects of water, to which we were now subject, and redirected them toward the greater good of our salvation in Jesus Christ. This began with the Great Flood in Genesis 6 through 9. As humanity had suffered near-complete spiritual death from its sins (Gen 6:5), so likewise did it suffer near-complete natural death from a flood in which the waters below and the waters above were set loose upon them (Gen 7:11). Yet just as Adam and Eve's sin did not result in the complete destruction of the human race but occasioned out of God's mercy the promise of a savior, so our subsequent sins did not result in the complete destruction of the human race by flood. The very waters that brought about the death of sinners also brought about the death of their *sins*; the Great Flood purified and renewed the human race through the righteousness of Noah and through the perseverance of his family on the ark (Gen 6:9, 11–22; 1 Pet 3:18–21).

God's use of water to point out the state of humanity's relationship to him continued in the Exodus. Having gathered the descendants of Noah through Abraham into a righteous family, the people of Israel, and having seen this family oppressed by the sins of their captors, the Egyptians, God determined once again to put an end to the oppression of his people by using water (Exod 2:24). In the First Plague, God turned the waters below from the Nile into blood to show the Egyptians that he was the Lord of creation (Exod 7:20); in the Seventh Plague, he formed the waters above into hail that rained down and killed both men and animals to show the Egyptians that, as the Lord of creation, he possessed power and glory (Exod 9:23). Finally, God liberated the people by a definitive action: he parted the Red Sea, allowed the Israelites to walk across it on dry land, and let the waters fall back upon the Egyptians and drown them (Exod 14:21–29). As the waters of the Great Flood gave death not only to the bulk of humanity but also to their sins, so likewise did the waters of the Red Sea give death not only to the Egyptians but also to the sins by which they bound the Israelites. Like the Great Flood, the parting of the Red Sea entailed a destruction of sin and a purification of the people who passed through it (1 Cor 10:2).

New Testament

|| ASSIGNED READING
|| Matthew 3

When God became man in Jesus Christ, he continued to use water to point out the state of his relationship with humanity. This began with the

25

baptism of Jesus in the Jordan River by John the Baptist. John the Baptist's baptism was not the same as the Christian Sacrament of Baptism (CCC 720). Like the signs of the Old Testament, it pointed to something but it did not make that thing happen: repentance. People came to John, they confessed their sins, and John washed them as a sign of repentance (Matt 3:6; Mark 1:4–5; Luke 3:3). But it was perfectly possible to undergo John's baptism without repenting from anything—in fact, that's just what the Pharisees and Sadducees tried to do (See Matt 3:7–10; Luke 3:7–9).

Since Jesus is God, and since God cannot lie, cheat, or deceive, Jesus underwent John's baptism with *real* repentance, unlike the Pharisees and Sadducees. Yet Jesus had nothing to repent from because he was entirely sinless (CCC 602). How, then, could Jesus repent? Jesus truly repented, but he repented for *our* sins, not his. His repentance in John's baptism was similar to his suffering on the Cross. He didn't repent *instead* of us; he repented as the *first* of us (CCC 618).

As Jesus passed through the waters of the Jordan River, a similar thing took place as had taken place in the Great Flood and the Crossing of the Red Sea: sin was crushed behind him and a purification of humanity took place. This is reflected in the way that Jesus relates to the water: "And when Jesus was baptized, he went up immediately from the water, and behold, the heavens were opened and he saw the Spirit of God descending like a dove" (Matt 3:16). Notice how Jesus does not suffer from any of the dangers that we do because of the Fall. He is immersed in the *waters below*, like the Egyptians, but the waters do not drown him. The heavens are opened in the *waters above*, like in the time of Noah, but there is no flood. Instead, there is only the grace of the Holy Spirit in the form of a dove, and the voice of the Father: "This is my beloved Son, with whom I am well pleased" (Matt 3:17). Jesus is in perfect friendship and fellowship with the Father and the Holy Spirit; his baptism represents the purification of humanity so that it can share with him in the life of God.

It is only when Jesus takes not only our *repentance* upon himself but also suffers the principal *punishment* for our sins on the Cross that we hear him suffer from the ill effects of water and say, "I thirst" (John 19:28). This is a surprising remark from someone who had earlier said, "whoever drinks of the water that I shall give him will never thirst; the water that I shall give him will become in him a spring of water welling up to eternal life" (John 4:14). Are we to understand that Jesus had succumbed completely to our sins? Far from it! No sooner had Jesus suffered from our thirst than he showed that there was in him a superabundance of water: the water of life, empowered by his blood, flowing from his pierced side (John 19:34; CCC 766, 1225). His thirst was for souls; if there was any water lacking in him, it was because he poured it all out for us.

Since Jesus suffered as the *first* of us, but not *instead* of us, Jesus asked his disciples to take up their crosses and follow him (Matt 10:38; 16:24; Mark 8:34; Luke 9:23; CCC 618). Following his Resurrection, he told them to go out into the world and conform all would-be followers to that same pattern of life. In order to empower them to do that, he gave them the Sacrament of Baptism. Thus Jesus spoke to his disciples, "All authority in heaven and on earth has been given to me. Go therefore and make disciples of all nations, baptizing them in the name of the Father and of the Son and of the Holy Spirit" (Matt 28:18–19).

The disciples listened. On the day of Pentecost, when Peter preached the saving work of Jesus and the crowds asked him and the other Apostles, "Brethren, what shall we do?" Peter replied, "Repent, and be baptized every one of you in the name of Jesus Christ for the forgiveness of your sins; and you shall receive the gift of the Holy Spirit" (Acts 2:37–38).

History and Theology

|| ASSIGNED READING
|| CCC 1210–1284

Following the command of Jesus and the example of the early Church, the Catholic Church teaches that Baptism is necessary for salvation:

> The Lord himself affirms that Baptism is necessary for salvation [Cf. *Jn* 3:5]. He also commands his disciples to proclaim the Gospel to all nations and to baptize them [Cf. *Mt* 28:19-20; cf. Council of Trent (1547) DS 1618; *LG* 14; *AG* 5]. Baptism is

necessary for salvation for those to whom the Gospel has been proclaimed and who have had the possibility of asking for this sacrament [Cf. *Mk* 16:16]. The Church does not know of any means other than Baptism that assures entry into eternal beatitude; this is why she takes care not to neglect the mission she has received from the Lord to see that all who can be baptized are "reborn of water and the Spirit." *God has bound salvation to the sacrament of Baptism, but he himself is not bound by his sacraments.* (CCC 1257)

This does not mean that every single person who makes it to heaven will have received the Sacrament of Baptism here on earth, however. Already in the early Church we have an example of people who received the Holy Spirit and the grace of Baptism without actually having been baptized, because their hearts were moved to true repentance by Peter's preaching (Acts 10:44–46). Not that this in any way minimizes Jesus' command—the Scriptures tell us that, in obedience to Jesus' command to baptize all the world, Peter commanded those who had received the Holy Spirit to be baptized all the same (Acts 10:47–48). Nevertheless, if God can give the grace of Baptism outside the celebration of the Sacrament of Baptism, one may rightfully ask: how or when does God do so?

The Catechism passage referenced above points to the first thing we must keep in mind if we want to know how or when God gives people baptismal grace outside of Baptism: we do not know for certain anything about the mystery of God's will unless he tells us.[1] Moreover, God told us in Jesus' command that he wills that all people should be baptized. There are, therefore, only two things concerning Baptism about which we can be absolutely sure: (1) everyone needs to be baptized; (2) if someone is baptized, God is offering that person the grace of salvation.

Outside of what we can be absolutely sure about, there are some things about which we may speculate or for which we may hope. The first of these is the salvation of those who die while they are still preparing for Baptism.

---

[1] Aquinas, ST Ia, q. 1, a. 1.

In the first centuries of the Church, Christian initiation saw considerable development. A long period of catechumenate included a series of preparatory rites, which were liturgical landmarks along the path of catechumenal preparation and culminated in the celebration of the sacraments of Christian initiation (CCC 1229).

After the Second Vatican Council, the Church restored the catechumenate through the Rite of Christian Initiation for Adults (RCIA). It is a process, typically lasting a year, during which a person is instructed in the faith, accepts the Gospel, professes the faith, and ultimately receives the Sacraments of Initiation (CCC 1229). This means that in the ancient Church and in the Church today there may be a considerable length of time between when a person formally asks for Baptism and when that person is ultimately baptized. What if someone should die during that time?

The question is an old one. It was addressed in the ancient Church by St. Ambrose, Bishop of Milan, concerning the Roman Emperor Valentinian II. Valentinian wanted to be baptized and he asked Ambrose to baptize him, but he got sick and died before Ambrose could do so. In his funeral oration for the deceased emperor, Ambrose said:

> But I hear you lamenting the fact that he did not receive the ceremonies of Baptism.[2] Tell me: what else can we do except desire [to be baptized] and request [Baptism]? Yet he already had the specific desire to receive the sacraments of initiation before he came into Italy: he recently noted that he wanted to be baptized by me, and therefore above all else he asked me to come to him. Does he not therefore have the grace which he desired? Does he not have the grace which he sought? Indeed, since he sought it, he received it. And it is written: "from whatever death the just man has suffered, his soul shall be at rest" (Wis. 7:4). Therefore, O Holy Father, absolve . . . your servant Valentinian of this obligation; the obligation which he desired to fulfill, the obligation

---

[2] Ambrose uses the word *sacramenta* not to mean "sacraments" but to mean "signs"; hence it has been translated "ceremonies."

which he reasonably and firmly sought to fulfill while yet alive. If he delayed because he was sick, still, deep down he was never a stranger to your mercy; he was beguiled by the swift passing of time, not his desire.[3]

Ambrose reasons that since Valentinian did everything within his power, desiring Baptism and requesting it from the Church, and since he did not hesitate or waver in that desire or that request (he was detained by illness, but who could blame him for that?), a merciful God would not refuse to give him the grace that he would have otherwise received in Baptism, even if through no fault of his own he was prevented from actually being baptized.

The Church has followed Ambrose's reasoning. Although we can never be absolutely certain about whether a particular catechumen really had an unwavering desire for Baptism and really did not delay in requesting it from the Church (only God knows our hearts), we can be absolutely certain that *if* he or she had an unwavering desire and *if* he or she did not delay in requesting Baptism from the Church, then God would not refuse to offer him or her the grace of Baptism without the Sacrament of Baptism.

Receiving baptismal grace in this way is called a "Baptism of Desire" (CCC 1259). A Baptism of Desire is not a Baptism properly speaking (CCC 1258). We call it Baptism analogously because it is an occasion on which God might choose to offer someone the same grace that they would have received if they had been baptized. A person who receives a Baptism of Desire can go to heaven because they have received the forgiveness of their sins and friendship with God, but that person isn't baptized because they were never washed with water in the way that Jesus commanded the Church. Catechumens are not the only ones who can receive a Baptism of Desire. Anyone who seeks the truth sincerely and does the will of God diligently can be saved in the same way (CCC 1260).

If anyone who seeks the truth sincerely and does the will of God diligently can be saved, all the more so can those who suffer death for Christ

---

[3] Ambrose, *De obitu Valentiniani* 51 (CSEL 73:354).

before being baptized. The Church teaches that these people receive a "Baptism of Blood," which, like a Baptism of Desire, is not Baptism properly speaking; we call it Baptism analogously because it is an occasion on which God might choose to offer someone baptismal grace without the Sacrament of Baptism (CCC 1258).

As with the case of a Baptism of Desire, we can never be absolutely sure that a particular individual received a Baptism of Blood because we can never be absolutely sure that, before Baptism, a particular individual believed and acted in such a way that God would offer them the grace of Baptism. But we can be absolutely sure that *if* they had an unwavering faith and *if* they offered themselves and were killed out of others' hatred for faith in Christ, then God would not refuse to offer them baptismal grace without the Sacrament of Baptism.

The most delicate and sensitive question about Baptism concerns the fate of those children who die without Baptism before they are old enough either to desire and request Baptism or to offer their lives for faith in Christ. Such children include those who die of miscarriages, abortions, stillbirths, and by any means after birth before they reach the age of reason. Traditionally, it was thought that such children go to a place called "Limbo," where they are separated from the vision of God because they were still subject to original sin when they died, but do not suffer from any torments because they did not commit any personal sins when they were alive; they enjoy a life of happiness and contemplation, but not of supernatural friendship and fellowship with God.

In spite of that longstanding opinion, however, there is reason to hope that these children, like adults, may be able to obtain a Baptism of Desire or a Baptism of Blood and so go to heaven instead. In the first case, the Church has approved a funeral liturgy for the children of parents who intended to present them for Baptism; in the second case, the Church celebrates the Feast of the Holy Innocents, who were killed on account of Christ while they were all below the age of reason.[4]

---

[4] International Theological Commission, *The Hope of Salvation for Infants who Die without being Baptized* (2007), no. 5, http://www.vatican.va/roman_curia/congregations/cfaith/cti_documents/rc_con_cfaith_doc_20070419_un-baptised-infants_en.html.

Apart from a reasonable hope that unbaptized children may receive a Baptism of Desire or a Baptism of Blood,

> the Church can only entrust them to the mercy of God, as she does in her funeral rites for them. Indeed, the great mercy of God who desires that all men should be saved, and Jesus' tenderness toward children which caused him to say: "Let the children come to me, do not hinder them" [*Mk* 10:14; cf. *1 Tim* 2:4], allow us to hope that there is a way of salvation for children who have died without Baptism. All the more urgent is the Church's call not to prevent little children coming to Christ through the gift of holy Baptism. (CCC 1261)

So, while Baptism is necessary for salvation, there may yet be many people in heaven who were never baptized: those who received a Baptism of Desire and those who received a Baptism of Blood.

QUESTIONS FOR REVIEW

1. Before the Fall, what could Adam and Eve learn from water about their relationship with God?
2. After the Fall, how did God use water to bring about purification from sin? Give two examples.
3. Why was Jesus baptized?
4. Is Baptism necessary for salvation?
5. What is a Baptism of Desire? What is a Baptism of Blood?

QUESTIONS FOR DISCUSSION

1. How can the baptism of Jesus help us think about the relationship that God wants to have with us in our own baptism?
2. Why do some people have a hard time with the idea that Baptism is necessary for salvation? How can you best respond?

Chapter 2

LIVING THE SACRAMENT

|| ASSIGNED READING
|| CIC, Canons 849–878

Celebration

What is necessary for salvation is conveyed at the central moment of Baptism. In that moment, the minister of the sacrament says, "N., I baptize you in the name of the Father, and of the Son, and of the Holy Spirit";[1] at the mention of each person of the Holy Trinity, he either immerses the candidate in water or pours water over that person's head (CCC 1239).

The minister of Baptism is ordinarily a bishop, priest, or deacon (CCC 1256; CIC, Canon 861, §1); since Baptism incorporates a person into a Christian community, it should usually be administered by the pastor of the parish where a person lives (CIC, Canon 530, § 1), or in the case of adult converts, the bishop of the diocese (CIC, Canon 863).

The candidate for Baptism, if they have reached the age of reason and are not in danger of death, "must have manifested the intention to receive baptism, have been instructed sufficiently about the truths of the

---

[1] N. stands for *Name*. The minister recites the person's first name and any middle names, but not his or her last name.

faith and Christian obligations, and have been tested in the Christian life through the Catechumenate" (CIC, Canon 865, §1).

If, on the other hand, the candidate has not reached the age of reason and is not in danger of death, at least one parent or person legitimately taking their place must consent to their baptism, and "there must be a founded hope that the infant will be brought up in the Catholic religion" (CIC, Canon 868).

Owing to the fact that Baptism is necessary for salvation, the Church dispenses with almost every rule about it in danger of death. If someone is in danger of death, any person can serve as a minister of Baptism even if that person has not yet been baptized, provided that they wash the one who is in danger of death three times with water while reciting the Trinitarian formula, as in the central moment of Baptism, and intend to do what the Church does when she baptizes (CCC 1256). All that is required in a recipient in danger of death is that "having some knowledge of the principal truths of the faith, the person has manifested in any way at all the intention to receive Baptism and promises to observe the commandments of the Christian religion" (CIC, Canon 865, §2). No express desire is necessary in the case of infants who are in danger of death. Owing to the importance of Baptism for salvation and the uncertainty of their state, they should be baptized right away and may even be baptized against the will of their parents (CIC, Canon 867, §2; 868, §2).

Outside of the danger of death, the Church celebrates the Sacrament of Baptism with a number of signs and ceremonies, which enrich the central moment and help us to celebrate it more reverently. While these signs and symbols are not necessary for salvation like Baptism is, it is fitting that we should observe them because they prepare us to benefit as much as possible from the graces offered to us at that central moment of the sacrament.[2]

First, the celebration begins with the Sign of the Cross, by which we are reminded of what Jesus did to make possible our reception of his Spirit through Baptism (CCC 1235). It continues with the proclamation of the Word of God, by which the candidates for Baptism are enlightened

---

[2] Aquinas, ST IIIa, q. 83, a. 4, ad 1.

with the truth of the Gospel and give evidence of the faith they wish to receive when they are baptized (CCC 1236). Then follows one or more exorcisms, through which the candidates are prepared to receive the Holy Spirit by liberation from the devil, and after which they renounce the devil explicitly (CCC 1237). Next, a prayer is said to consecrate the water in which the candidates will be baptized by calling down the Holy Spirit upon it (CCC 1238).

Only after the candidate has been reminded of the Cross that made Baptism possible, enlightened by the Revelation of what Jesus calls us to in Baptism, liberated from the devil who seeks to prevent Baptism, and only after the Holy Spirit has been called down upon the water to confer Baptism, does the central moment of Baptism take place.

Through the gift of the Holy Spirit, Baptism incorporates us into Christ. For this reason, there follows an anointing with sacred chrism, which recalls the anointings of prophets, priests, and kings in the Old Testament (Exod 28:41) and signifies that the baptized person has been made a sharer in Christ's prophetic, priestly, and kingly offices (CCC 1241). Finally, the newly baptized person is given two symbolic gifts: a white garment, symbolizing the purity of soul that the person has received by "putting on Christ," and a candle, symbolizing that by putting on Christ the person has been enlightened by the faith of the Gospel (CCC 1243).

What we have said thus far applies to adults. In the early Church, adult baptisms made up the majority of baptisms, since the majority of converts were either Jewish adults who found the fulfillment of their expectations in Christ or Gentile adults who heard about Christ and sought salvation in him. But with the passing of generations, as more and more adults were incorporated into Christ through Baptism, it was only natural that they should seek for their children the salvation in Christ that they themselves enjoyed. The Scriptures seem to bear witness to this fact when they mention the baptism of entire "households," which would have included children (CCC 1252). Likewise, apostolic tradition from the second century attests to the fact that the baptism of children was an ordinary feature of the Christian life (CCC 1252).

When children are baptized, they do not go through the entire year-long process that adults do. Instead, the Church abridges the ceremonies of Baptism into a single rite and reminds those responsible for the child of their duty to oversee the child's education in the Christian faith (CCC 1231, 1251).

The Church requires that Catholic parents have their children baptized within the first few weeks after birth (CIC, Canon 867, §1). This is in recognition of the fact that:

> Born with a fallen human nature and tainted by original sin, children also have need of the new birth in Baptism to be freed from the power of darkness and brought into the realm of the freedom of the children of God, to which all men are called [Cf. Council of Trent (1546): DS 1514; cf. *Col* 1:12–14]. . . . The Church and the parents would deny a child the priceless grace of becoming a child of God were they not to confer Baptism shortly after birth [Cf. CIC, can. 867; CCEO, cann. 681; 686, 1]. (CCC 1250)

The baptism of children is not done in response to any desire or petition on the child's own part. Of their nature, children are unable to manifest desires at the level of reason; only at the level of basic life are they able to give some sign of their needs. Yet, just as in all other things, parents make decisions for the good of their children, so also in Baptism do parents, as members of the Church, profess the faith on behalf of their child.[3]

Parents, however, do not profess faith for their children alone. Rather, they do so with the support of the whole Christian community on earth and in heaven. In light of this, the Church also recognizes the role of godparents, who together with the child's parents take upon themselves the responsibility for the child's spiritual development. Since the post-baptismal catechesis of a child is the only way that a child can come to know the Catholic faith, the Church makes that catechesis a shared responsibility (CCC 1255).

---

[3] Pope Francis, Encyclical Letter on the Faith *Lumen fidei* (June 29, 2013), §43.

Effects of the Sacrament

As the foundation of the seven sacraments, Baptism marks a fundamentally new beginning in a person's life. This new beginning is so radical that Jesus describes it as a "re-birth" (John 3:5). Just like natural birth marks a whole set of new beginnings for a child—who can now breathe, eat, and be hugged by the parents—so also spiritual birth marks a whole set of new beginnings: forgiveness, spiritual life, grace, membership in the Church, fellowship with Christians, and an indelible mark that signifies one's adoption as a son or daughter of God.

The first new beginning that Baptism brings us is the forgiveness of sins (CCC 1263). At its heart, all sin is an "offense against God" that separates us from his love and friendship (CCC 1850). By uniting us with Jesus, who repented for our sins at his Baptism, and who made satisfaction for our sins on his Cross, Baptism reconciles us with God the Father by restoring us to the friendship and fellowship with God that Jesus never lost (CCC 977). For this reason, St. Paul says that Baptism makes us die and rise with Christ (see Rom 6:3–4; CCC 1227).

The first kind of sin that Baptism forgives is *original sin*. Original sin is the consequence of the first sin by which Adam and Eve fell from God's friendship and fellowship. God had given Adam and Eve two gifts that he intended them to pass on to their children: original justice, by which their bodies listened to their souls, and holiness, by which their souls listened to God. Since Adam and Eve lost justice and holiness, all subsequent people are born outside of the kind of relationship with God that he originally intended.

Original sin is not a sin properly speaking. "Original sin is called 'sin' only in an analogical sense: it is a sin 'contracted' and not 'committed'—a state and not an act" (CCC 404). Baptism remedies original sin by restoring us to a state of holiness so that we may enjoy the friendship and fellowship that God intended for us from the beginning. It does not, however, restore the fullness of justice; it restores our *ability* to act justly without restoring our inclination to act justly. There remains in us after Baptism "an inclination to sin that Tradition calls *concupiscence*, or metaphorically, 'the tinder for sin' (*fomes peccati*)" (CCC 1264). That might sound scary, but it is actually good news. Since God gives us the ability to overcome this inclination, if we do so successfully it actually increases our holiness beyond what Adam and Eve had (CCC 1264; see also CCC 978).

In addition to original sin, Baptism also forgives any *personal sins* we may have committed (CCC 1263). Personal sins are actions that we undertake purposefully that wound our relationship with God. There are two kinds of personal sin. The first is mortal sin, which occurs when we violate one of the Ten Commandments with full knowledge and deliberate consent. Mortal sin alienates us from God. The second kind, venial sin, occurs when we commit some offense against God in which we do not violate one of the Ten Commandments; or we do so but are inculpably ignorant of the fact and/or we commit the sin without deliberate consent. Venial sin wounds our relationship with God without alienating us from him (CCC 1855–1864).

By joining us to the Cross of Jesus, Baptism forgives all personal sins whatsoever and all punishment for them. If we were to die immediately after Baptism, there would be nothing to stop us from going straight to heaven.

The second new beginning that Baptism brings is life as a new creature (CCC 1265). That doesn't mean that God destroys who we were and makes us into a completely new person. Rather, it means that God does something that is new to us personally, but that is not new to the human race. He sends us his Holy Spirit, so that we become what Adam and Eve were: "Adopted son[s] of God . . . 'partaker[s] of the divine nature' [2 Cor 5:17; 2 Pet 1:4; cf. Gal 4:5–7], member[s] of Christ and co-heir[s] with him, and . . . temple[s] of the Holy Spirit [Cf. 1 Cor 6:15; 12:27; Rom 8:17]" (CCC 1265). Rather than making us into different people, this makes us into the very people that God wanted us to be all along. It does so by marking a third new beginning: the beginning of the presence of sanctifying grace.

As mentioned above, sanctifying grace is the principal effect on us when the Holy Spirit dwells in our souls. It includes with it all sorts of other gifts from God with which he would like to enrich us: the theological virtues, the Gifts of the Holy Spirit, and the infused moral virtues (CCC 1266).

By incorporating us into Christ, forgiving our sins, giving us the Holy Spirit, and filling us with sanctifying grace, Baptism also gives us a fourth new beginning: membership in the Body of Christ, which is the Church. As we saw above, no one in Scripture was ever baptized alone. People were baptized by a member of the Church, and by their Baptism they joined in fellowship with the Church.

St. Paul tells us that being a member of the Body of Christ entails four things, which are necessary for the good of any body: unity, cooperation, contribution, and coordination. Through our Baptism, we get to be fully *united* with the other members of the Body, we need to *cooperate* with them for the good of the whole, we have the opportunity to *contribute* our particular gifts to the Body, and we must *coordinate* with them under the direction of the leaders in authority over us (1 Cor 12:12–31; CCC 1267–1269). In addition, we also gain an imperfect but real association with those who, while baptized, are not in full communion with the Church (CCC 1271).

As a sign and seal of all the other new beginnings, Baptism imparts one final gift to us: that of an indelible spiritual mark that not even sin can destroy, which is always visible to God, and which will be visible to all the saints in heaven. That spiritual mark is called a *character*.

The word "character" is a Greek word. Originally, it referred to a stamp, a seal (which was made with a stamp), or a branding (which was made by stamping someone or something with a hot iron). In the Roman Empire soldiers were branded with a hot iron as a mark of their service. The branding caused a permanent scar. That scar prevented people from deserting the army when times got tough, because deserting soldiers could always be identified.

Just as Tertullian made an association between the sacraments and the oath to enter Roman military service, so also Augustine made an association between the branding that Roman soldiers received and the seal that Baptism imprints:

If anyone, whether a deserter or someone who had never served in the military at all, brands some civilian with the military mark, when it is discovered isn't the one who has been branded punished as a deserter, and all the more severely to the extent that it proves that he had never fought at all, while, if he betrays him, the one who so audaciously branded him is punished along with him? Or, if perhaps the one who hadn't fought was terrified, and, shuddering at that character of the military, took refuge in the mercy of the emperor, and, after having poured out his entreaty and been granted pardon, he then began to fight, when the man had been freed and corrected, would the character really be repeated and not rather acknowledged and approved? Or do Christian sacraments hold fast less than this bodily mark . . . ? Or should we not make a comparison with the military, when the Apostle both mentions competitive struggles and openly cries, "no one, who fights for God, entangles himself with civilian pursuits, so that he may please the one who recruited him" (2 Tim. 2:4)?[4]

Following Augustine's reasoning, the Church recognizes that three sacraments—Baptism, Confirmation, and Holy Orders—imprint a character on the Christian soul, which can never be taken away; consequently these sacraments can never be repeated (CCC 698, 1295). The character of Baptism enables the Christian faithful to partake in the Church's liturgical worship of God, especially with regard to the other sacraments, and marks off a person as Christ's own on the day of redemption (CCC 1273–1274).

Appropriating and Living This Sacrament

The day of our Baptism is the day that spiritual life comes to be in us, the day when we are united to Christ crucified, our sins are washed away, the Holy Spirit comes to dwell in us, sanctifying grace is poured into our souls, we are grafted on as members of Christ's body, and an indelible character is impressed on our souls to mark us as Christ's own forever. It is, in short, our spiritual birthday. If, therefore, our natural birth is cause

---

[4] Augustine, *Contra epistolam Parmeniani* 2.13.29 (CSEL 51:80–81).

for a yearly celebration, how much more so should our spiritual birth be the cause of a continual reminder, an ever-deepening contemplation, and a never-ending transformation of our lives as we grow in Christ.

The Church recognizes how important it is for us to remember and to celebrate our Baptism, and so she provides a number of "sacramentals" for this purpose. Sacramentals are not sacraments; they are instituted by the Church and not necessarily by Christ. They exist not as a replacement for sacraments but to dispose us to participate in the sacraments well. Even though they are not sacraments, sacramentals can still give us grace. They do so not because they involve the words of Christ but because they involve the prayer of the Church (CCC 1670), which Christ promised to hear (CCC 1088).

The first and foremost of the sacramentals that recall Baptism is the blessing of the baptismal water at the Easter Vigil. In this celebration, as the Church prepares for catechumens to be reborn, she asks everyone to recall with thanksgiving the moment when Christ gave them the same rebirth. She does so first by recounting the whole biblical history leading up to Baptism: Creation, the Great Flood, the Red Sea, the baptism of Jesus, his command to baptize all nations, and the sending of his Holy Spirit (CCC 1217–1222). Following the memory of these events, the Church welcomes all the baptized to relive them by the renewal of their baptismal promises (CCC 1254). In order to draw everyone more deeply into the celebration of Baptism, the priest then sprinkles all the faithful with the baptismal water, a rite that can be repeated at the start of any Mass or called to mind any time we cross ourselves with Holy Water at the entrance to a Church or to our homes (CCC 1668).

The sacramentals of the Church help us to remember our own baptism, but they are not just reminders of the past. They help us to enter more deeply into the present life of grace that Baptism has given us. As mentioned above, that life entails a sharing in Christ's priestly, prophetic, and kingly offices (CCC 871, 873, 897, 1241, 1291). The baptized share in the kingly and priestly offices of Christ because—as people who have been united to the Cross of Christ and who have received the forgiveness of sins, the Holy Spirit, and sanctifying grace—they are capable of ruling over themselves and their desires, offering themselves as a spiritual sacrifice to God in their worship and throughout their daily lives (CCC 1268).[5] The baptized share in the prophetic office of Christ because, by the sacrificial offering of themselves to God, they form "a living witness" to him.[6]

> So also are you yourself made king and priest and prophet in the Laver; a king, having dashed to earth all the deeds of wickedness and slain your sins; a priest, in that you offer yourself to God, having sacrificed your body and being yourself slain also, for if we died with Him, says he, we shall also live with Him (2 Timothy 2:11); a prophet, knowing what shall be, and being inspired of God.[7]

In this way, the Christian life follows the pattern of the life of God's people from the beginning of redemption. With water having destroyed our sins, God calls us to an ever-deeper share in the grace of Christ. The more we live out that calling, the more we grow in the graces offered to us by the Sacrament of Baptism and the more the truth of God's saving actions is proclaimed through our deeds.

SELECTED READING
Cyril of Jerusalem, *Mystagogical Catechesis* 1

I have long been wishing, O true-born and dearly beloved children of the Church, to discourse to you concerning these spiritual and heavenly Mysteries; but since I well knew that seeing is far more persuasive than hearing, I waited for the present season; that finding you more open to the influence of my words from your present experience, I might lead you by the hand into the brighter and more fragrant meadow of the Paradise before us; especially as you have been

---

[5] Second Vatican Council, Dogmatic Constitution on the Church *Lumen Gentium* (November 21, 1964), §10

[6] Second Vatican Council, *Lumen Gentium*, §11.

[7] St. John Chrysostom, *Homilies on 2 Corinthians* 3.7 (NPNF 12:293).

made fit to receive the more sacred Mysteries, after having been found worthy of divine and life-giving Baptism. Since therefore it remains to set before you a table of the more perfect instructions, let us now teach you these things exactly, that you may know the effect wrought upon you on that evening of your baptism.

First ye entered into the vestibule of the Baptistery, and there facing towards the West ye listened to the command to stretch forth your hand, and as in the presence of Satan ye renounced him. Now ye must know that this figure is found in ancient history. For when Pharaoh, that most bitter and cruel tyrant, was oppressing the free and high-born people of the Hebrews, God sent Moses to bring them out of the evil bondage of the Egyptians. Then the door posts were anointed with the blood of a lamb, that the destroyer might flee from the houses which had the sign of the blood; and the Hebrew people was marvellously delivered. The enemy, however, after their rescue, *pursued after them* (Exodus 14:9, 23), and saw the sea wondrously parted for them; nevertheless he went on, following close in their footsteps, and was all at once overwhelmed and engulfed in the Red Sea.

Now turn from the old to the new, from the figure to the reality. There we have Moses sent from God to Egypt; here, Christ, sent forth from His Father into the world: there, that Moses might lead forth an afflicted people out of Egypt; here, that Christ might rescue those who are oppressed in the world under sin: there, the blood of a lamb was the spell against the destroyer; here, the blood of the Lamb without blemish Jesus Christ is made the charm to scare evil spirits: there, the tyrant was pursuing that ancient people even to the sea; and here the daring and shameless spirit, the author of evil, was following you even to the very streams of salvation. The tyrant of old was drowned in the sea; and this present one disappears in the water of salvation.

But nevertheless you are bidden to say, with arm outstretched towards him as though he were present, *"I renounce you, Satan."* I wish also to say wherefore ye stand facing to the West; for it is necessary. Since the West is the region of sensible darkness, and he being darkness has his dominion also in darkness, therefore, looking with a symbolic meaning towards the West, you renounce that dark and gloomy potentate. What then did each of you stand up and say? *I renounce you, Satan,*—you wicked and most cruel tyrant! Meaning, *I fear your might no longer; for that Christ has overthrown, having partaken with me of flesh and blood, that through these He might by death destroy death (Hebrews 2:14–15), that I might not be made subject to bondage forever. I renounce you,*—you crafty and most subtle serpent. *I renounce you,*—plotter as you are, who under the guise of friendship contrived all disobedience, and work apostasy in our first parents. *I renounce you, Satan,*—the artificer and abettor of all wickedness.

Then in a second sentence you are taught to say, *"and all your works."* Now the works of Satan are all sin, which also you must renounce — just as one who has escaped a tyrant has surely escaped his weapons also. All sin therefore, of every kind, is included in the works of the devil. Only know this; that all that you say, especially at that most thrilling hour, is written in God's books; when therefore you do any thing contrary to these promises, you shall be judged as a *transgressor* (Galatians 2:18). You renounce therefore the works of Satan; I mean, all deeds and thoughts which are contrary to reason.

Then you say, *"And all his pomp."* Now the pomp of the devil is the madness of theatres, and horse-races, and hunting, and all such vanity: from which that holy man praying to be delivered says unto God, *Turn away my eyes from beholding vanity.* Be not interested in the madness of the theatre, where you will behold the wanton gestures of the players , carried on with mockeries and all unseemliness, and the frantic dancing of effeminate men—nor in the madness of them who in hunts expose themselves to wild beasts, that they may pamper their miserable appetite; who, to serve their belly with meats, become themselves in reality meat for the belly of untamed beasts; and to speak justly, for the sake of their own god, their belly, they cast away their life headlong in single combats. Shun also horse-races, that frantic and soul-subverting spectacle. For all these are the pomp of the devil.

Moreover, the things which are hung up at idol festivals, either meat or bread, or other such things polluted by the invocation of the unclean spirits, are reckoned in the pomp of the devil. For as the Bread and Wine of the Eucharist before the invocation of the Holy and Adorable Trinity were simple bread and wine, while after the invocation the Bread becomes the Body of Christ, and the Wine the Blood of Christ, so in like manner such meats belonging to the pomp of Satan, though in their own nature simple, become profane by the invocation of the evil spirit.

After this you say, *"and all your service."* Now the service of the devil is prayer in idol temples; things done in honour of lifeless idols; the lighting of lamps, or burning of incense by fountains or rivers, as some persons cheated by dreams or by evil spirits do [resort to this], thinking to find a cure even for their bodily ailments. Go not after such things. The watching of birds, divination, omens, or amulets, or charms written on leaves, sorceries, or other evil arts, and all such things, are services of the devil; therefore shun them. For if after renouncing Satan and associating yourself with Christ, thou fall under their influence, you shall find the tyrant more bitter; perchance, because he treated you of old as his own, and relieved you from his hard bondage, but has now been greatly exasperated by you; so you will be bereaved of Christ, and have experience of the other. Have you not heard the old history which tells us of Lot and his daughters? Was not he himself saved with his daughters, when he had gained the mountain, while his wife became a pillar of salt, set up as a monument for ever, in remembrance of her depraved will and her turning back. Take heed therefore to yourself, and turn not again to *what is behind*, having put your hand to the plough, and then turning back to the salt savour of this life's doings; but escape to the mountain, to Jesus Christ, that *stone hewn without hands* (Daniel 2:35, 45), which has filled the world.

When therefore you renounce Satan, utterly breaking all your covenant with him, that ancient *league with hell* (Isaiah 28:15), there is opened to you the paradise of God, which He planted towards the East, whence for his transgression our first father was banished; and a symbol of this was your turning from West to East, the place of light. Then you were told to say, "*I believe in the Father, and in the Son, and in the Holy Ghost, and in one Baptism of repentance.*" Of which things we spoke to you at length in the former Lectures, as God's grace allowed us.

Guarded therefore by these discourses, *be sober. For our adversary the devil,* as was just now read, *as a roaring lion, walks about, seeking whom he may devour* (1 Peter 5:9). But though in former times death was mighty and devoured, at the holy Laver of regeneration God has *wiped away every tear from off all faces.* For you shall no more mourn, now that you have put off the old man; but you shall keep holy-day, *clothed in the garment of salvation* (Isaiah 61:10), even Jesus Christ.

QUESTIONS FOR REVIEW

1. What are the necessary words that must be spoken in Baptism?
2. Who ordinarily administers the sacrament? Are there any exceptions to this?
3. What types of sins are forgiven in Baptism?
4. What "new beginnings" does Baptism mark?
5. What do we call the spiritual mark Baptism leaves on us? Can that mark ever be taken away?

QUESTIONS FOR DISCUSSION

1. Do you remember your baptism day? If so, what was special about it? If not, or if you have not yet been baptized, have you been to someone else's baptism? What seemed special about it?
2. What are some ways you can call upon the graces you received on your baptism day? If you have not already been baptized, why do you think the Church urges people to do this?

Part III

CONFIRMATION

Confirmation is the second of the seven sacraments, as well as the second Sacrament of Initiation. Its name comes from the Latin word *confirmatio*, which does not mean "confirming" so much as it means "strengthening" or "fortifying." In the most basic form of Confirmation, a bishop says to the person who is going to be confirmed, "Be sealed with the Gift of the Holy Spirit," and imposes his hand on the forehead of the person who is to be confirmed while anointing him or her with chrism oil (CCC 1300; CIC, Canon 880, §1).[1]

> The sacrament of confirmation strengthens the baptized and obliges them more firmly to be witnesses of Christ by word and deed and to spread and defend the faith. It imprints a character, enriches by the gift of the Holy Spirit the baptized continuing on the path of Christian Initiation, and binds them more perfectly to the Church. (CIC, Canon 879)

---

[1] In the East, other parts of the body are anointed as well, and the minister of the sacrament, who is ordinarily a priest, announces with each anointing, "The seal of the gift of the Holy Spirit."

Chapter 1

Understanding the Sacrament

Old Testament

|| Assigned Reading
|| Exodus 30:22–28

Like water, oil was a common substance that was deeply embedded in the daily lives of the ancient Hebrews. First, it was food. The ancient Hebrews pressed olives and other fruits into oils much like we do today; then they cooked with the oil, making breads, cakes, and other dishes. Second, it was fuel. In the absence of electricity and petroleum products, they burned oil in their lamps to provide light. Third, it was a hygienic product. Oils could be used as a lotion following bathing; they could also be used to seal off wounds and protect against outside infection. Finally, it was an adornment. Owing to the sheen and suppleness that oil gives to our hair, our skin, and the things we make, oil could be used to make people and things more beautiful (CCC 1293).

Unlike water, oil was not immediately present at creation. Oil has to be made from things that require water for their growth. But when it is made, it is delicious, useful, beneficial, and beautiful. In a sense, therefore, oil brings perfection to water. Water nourishes us but doesn't taste like much or provide us with any calories; oil nourishes us, tastes good, and gives us energy. Water can power industry by day; oil gives light to the things that water powers by night and can be burned to power engines. Water makes athletes cool from the heat of exhaustion; in ancient times, oil made them slick so that their opponents could not hurt them. Bathing from dirt and washing wounds with water are essential to hygiene; moisturizing skin and sealing wounds with oil perfect it. Water makes things clean but dull and matted; it can also be infused with temporary scents like those of perfume and cologne. Oil makes clean things glisten with a beautiful sheen; it can be infused with much longer lasting scents than water can.

Because of the way in which oil perfects what water does, God decided to perfect with oil what he does with water. Yet, because every perfection that God gives to the world happens by the working of the Holy Spirit, the use of oil as a sign of perfection is always accompanied by a sign of the Holy Spirit.

After the Great Flood, which cleansed the world from sin, God sent Noah a dove with an olive leaf as a sign of the flood's completion (Gen 8:11). The appearance of a leaf from a tree indicated to Noah the completion of the flood and its effects; that it was a leaf from this kind of tree symbolized that God had once again adorned the world with oils for nourishment, natural and medicinal resources, and beauty. That the leaf was brought by a dove symbolizes to us that these gifts—nourishment, health, and beauty—come to us in the spiritual life from the Holy Spirit (CCC 701).

Similarly, after the crossing of the Red Sea, which freed the Israelites from the sins of the Egyptians and prepared the framework for the Mosaic Covenant, God commanded the Israelites to use oil as a symbol for how he was perfecting them as a people in his service. Since they reached the summit of their perfection in the worship of God, he asked them to make a special oil with which to anoint people and things that were to be consecrated to that service. That oil symbolized the Holy Spirit, and both people and things could be consecrated in it (CCC 609).

Three categories of people were anointed among the Israelites and each was empowered by the Holy Spirit for a specific purpose. Priests are the first to be mentioned in connection with holy oil (Exod 30:22–33). Priests were empowered by the Holy Spirit to offer ritual sacrifice on behalf of the people of Israel and assisted the people in living out their relationship with God (Exod 28–29; CCC 1539). Kings were also anointed with that oil (1 Sam 16:13). Kings were empowered by the Holy Spirit to govern Israel in such a way that the entire people assisted in their obedience to God through prayer (CCC 2579). Prophets were anointed as well (1 Kings 19:16). Prophets were empowered by the Holy Spirit to speak the words of God to the people of Israel, whether about the present or about the future (CCC 702).

In the course of history, God made a series of promises regarding the fulfillment of all three anointed offices: prophet, priest, and king. In each case, he promised a future servant who would discharge that anointed office in perfect faithfulness.

To the people under Moses, God promised to raise up a new prophet:

I will raise up for them a prophet like you from among their brethren; and I will put my words in his mouth, and he shall speak to them all that I command him. And whoever will not give heed to my words which he shall speak in my name, I myself will require it of him. But the prophet who presumes to speak a word in my name which I have not commanded him to speak, or who speaks in the name of other gods, that same prophet shall die. And if you say in your heart, "How may we know the word which the LORD has not spoken?"—when a prophet speaks in the name of the LORD, if the word does not come to pass or come true, that is a word which the LORD has not spoken; the prophet has spoken it presumptuously, you need not be afraid of him. (Deut 18:18–22)

To the people under Samuel, God promised to raise up a new priest:

And I will raise up for myself a faithful priest, who shall do according to what is in my heart and in my mind; and I will build him a sure house, and he shall go in and out before my anointed for ever. (1 Sam 2:35)

To the people under David, God promised to raise up a new king:

I will raise up your offspring after you, who shall come forth from your body, and I will establish his kingdom. He shall build a house for my name, and I will establish the throne of his kingdom for ever. I will be his father, and he shall be my son. When he commits iniquity, I will chasten him with the rod of men, with the stripes of the sons of men; but I will not take my merciful love from him, as I took it from Saul, whom I put away from before you. And your house and your kingdom shall be made sure for ever before me; your throne shall be established for ever. (2 Sam 7:12–16)

In Hebrew, the word for "anointed person" is *Mashiach*, a word that survives in English as "Messiah." Over the course of the history of the people of Israel, they looked to God for an anointed one, a Messiah, who would fulfill the promise of a faithful prophet, priest, and king (CCC 711–716). The role of the Messiah was twofold: it was to establish himself in faithfulness to God forever, and to gather a people to himself who would worship the Lord—Jewish people from the land of Israel, Jewish people in exile abroad, and non-Jewish people from every nation. Since the Messiah was to be anointed with the Holy Spirit, it was promised that he would share that Holy Spirit with his people from all over the world and renew their hearts in the knowledge and the love of God (Isa 44:1–8; Jer 31:31–34; 33:14–26; Ezek 36:25–27; CCC 1287).

New Testament

The New Testament tells us that all of the messianic promises were fulfilled in Jesus. In the Acts of the Apostles, Peter quotes the promise of a prophet and applies it to Jesus (Acts 3:22). In the Letter to the Hebrews, Paul references the promise of a priest and applies it to Jesus (Heb 7:20–28), as well as the promise of a king (Heb 1:5). From the very beginning of the Gospels, the word "Christ" is applied to Jesus. "Christ" is the English form of the Greek word *Christos*. It is a direct translation of the Hebrew word *Mashiach* (CCC 436).

More dramatically, the Gospels show us what Peter and Paul proclaim. On the day of Jesus' baptism, as the waters of the New Flood closed behind Jesus in a sign of his undertaking repentance for our sins, the Holy Spirit came down upon Jesus in the form of a dove. This completed Jesus' washing by showing the world that he had been anointed by the Spirit to preach the Gospel (see Luke 4:18). It is such a significant event that all four Gospels record it precisely (Matt 3:16; Mark 1:10; Luke 3:22; John 1:32; see CCC 1286).

Just as Jesus was baptized as the first of us, not instead of us, so likewise was he clothed with the Holy Spirit as the first of us, not instead of us. He indicated that we would receive the Holy Spirit like him during his public ministry, when he promised to send his Holy Spirit upon the disciples after his Resurrection and Ascension (Luke 24:48–49; John 7:39; 14:15–31; 16:4–14; Acts 1:8). On the day of Pentecost, Jesus kept that promise. With the disciples and people from every nation gathered in Jerusalem, he poured out his Holy Spirit visibly upon the Church so that their spiritual washing in Baptism might be completed by a spiritual anointing in Confirmation (Acts 2:1–47; CCC 1287). The effect of the Spirit's descent was dramatic. The very disciples who (though personally and communally reconciled to Christ) were leading a hidden life of prayer (Acts 1:14) became empowered and emboldened to preach the Gospel in public by word and deed (Acts 2:14–36).

From that point forward, just as the disciples obeyed the command of Jesus to go forth and baptize all nations, they also fulfilled the promise of Jesus to pour out his Spirit upon all nations by laying hands on the newly baptized so as to confer on them the same Spirit of anointing that they themselves had received. Very often this action was connected with visible signs to help the disciples draw the connection between the Church's Pentecost and this, their own personal pentecost (Acts 8:15–17; 19:5–6; Heb 6:2; CCC 1289).

History and Theology

|| ASSIGNED READING
|| CCC 1285–1321

Like Baptism, Confirmation in the ancient Church was usually conferred upon adult converts on Easter Vigil as part of a single celebration in which new Christians were baptized, confirmed, and received the Eucharist. In this context, it was easy simply to explain Confirmation as the descent of the Holy Spirit on the newly baptized:

> Having been baptized into Christ, and put on Christ, you have been made conformable to the Son of God; for God having foreordained us unto adoption as sons, made us to be conformed to the body of Christ's glory. Having therefore become partakers of Christ, you are properly called Christs, and of you God said, "Touch not My Christs," or anointed. . . . But beware of supposing this to be plain ointment. For as the Bread of the Eucharist, after the invocation of the Holy Ghost, is mere bread no longer, but the Body of Christ, so also this holy ointment is no more simple ointment, nor (so to say) common, after invocation, but it is Christ's gift of grace, and, by the advent of the Holy Ghost, is made fit to impart His Divine Nature. Which ointment is symbolically applied to thy forehead and thy other senses; and while

thy body is anointed with the visible ointment, thy soul is sanctified by the Holy and life-giving Spirit.[1]

However, as in the case of Baptism, with passing generations there
was a need to initiate more and more children into the Christian faith.
This led to a theological question: Should infants be confirmed? Jesus
does not give us any express command about this, and so the question
had to be answered by the Church using theological reasoning.

The theological tradition has given us two sets of reflections upon
the purpose of the Sacrament of Confirmation. The first emphasizes
Confirmation as the completion of Baptism by conferring upon the
recipient an increase in the Gifts of the Holy Spirit:

> There follows a spiritual seal, which you heard read today;
> because after the font we still have to perform the "perfec-
> tion," when, at the invocation of the priest, the Holy Spirit is
> poured out, the Spirit of wisdom and understanding, the Spirit
> of counsel and strength, the Spirit of knowledge and piety, the
> Spirit of holy fear: these are, as it were, the seven virtues of the
> Spirit. (Is 11:2)[2]

The second emphasizes Confirmation as empowering people to bear
public witness for the faith and to engage in spiritual combat. This tradition was originally applied to an anointing that people received before
Baptism in anticipation of the power they would receive from the Holy
Spirit after Baptism:

> You were anointed as though you were Christ's athlete, as
> though you were going to fight the battle of this world. You pro-
> fessed the prizes of your contest. He who wins gains that for
> which he hoped, and you find the crown where you find the
> fight. You contend in the world, but you are crowned by Christ.

---

[1] Cyril of Jerusalem, *Mystagogical Catecheses* 3.1, 3 (NPNF 2.7:149–150).
[2] Ambrose, *De sacramentis* 3.8 (CSEL 73:42).

... Even if your reward is in heaven, the merit of your reward is earned here."[3]

In the East there was a tendency to emphasize that Confirmation is the completion of Baptism. Consequently, Catholics in the East confer Confirmation upon infants after they are baptized; their word for it is Chrismation. Since it is ordinarily the parish priest who confers Baptism upon infants, the responsibility for the Chrismation of infants was likewise transferred to the priest, who still has to use oil consecrated by a bishop. In the West there was a tendency to emphasize that, by completing Baptism, Confirmation raises us to spiritual maturity and prepares us for spiritual combat. With nothing standing in the way, therefore, of delaying the sacrament, it continued to be reserved to the bishop, but was separated from the celebration of Baptism so that it could be conferred by the bishop at a later date (CCC 1290–1292).

QUESTIONS FOR REVIEW

1. In the ancient world, what did oil symbolize?
2. In the Old Testament, what were the three categories of people anointed by oil and why were they anointed?
3. Who was anointed in the Gospels?
4. What is received in Confirmation?
5. For what do the gifts we receive in Confirmation prepare us?

QUESTIONS FOR DISCUSSION

1. Why do you think Christians need special graces to give witness to Jesus in the world? What can make giving this witness difficult?
2. Describe a situation you have been in where it was difficult to follow Jesus or be a good witness to him. What happened? How can asking the Holy Spirit for help strengthen you to face similar situations in the future?

---

[3] Ambrose, *De sacramentis* 1.2.4 (CSEL 73:17).

Chapter 2

Living the Sacrament

|| Assigned Reading
|| CIC, Canons 879–896

Celebration

What is necessary for the descent of the Holy Spirit happens at the central moment of Confirmation. In that moment the minister of the sacrament says, "Be sealed with the Gift of the Holy Spirit," and imposes his hand on the candidate's forehead while anointing him or her with chrism oil (CCC 1300; CIC, Canon 880, §1).

In the celebration of Confirmation, the original minister of the Sacrament of Confirmation is the bishop, so the bishop should confer this sacrament where possible:

> Bishops are the successors of the apostles. They have received the fullness of the sacrament of Holy Orders. The administration of this sacrament by them demonstrates clearly that its effect is to unite those who receive it more closely to the Church, to her apostolic origins, and to her mission of bearing witness to Christ. (CCC 1313)

Owing to custom, priests, and in particular pastors of parishes, have become the ordinary minister of this sacrament in the East; in the West, priests can serve as extraordinary ministers of this sacrament with the bishop's permission (CCC 1312–1313). Yet, even when priests confer Confirmation, they still have to use chrism consecrated by a bishop; this preserves the connection with the Apostles even in the absence of one of their successors (CCC 1297, 1312).

The candidate for Confirmation must be already baptized and should be instructed in the Christian faith, disposed to receive the graces offered to them by the sacrament, and capable of renewing their baptismal promises (CCC 1306; CIC, Canon 889). In the Latin Rite, those who were baptized as children should be confirmed at the age of discretion (CCC 1307; CIC, Canon 891).

Since Confirmation is part of the fullness of Christian Initiation and since living the fullness of the Christian life requires a complete initiation into the Christian religion, several consequences follow.

The first is that, while Confirmation is not necessary for salvation in the same way that Baptism is (CCC 1023, 1030, 1274), Confirmation nevertheless has its own kind of necessity, as St. Thomas Aquinas explains:

> All the sacraments are in some way necessary for salvation: for certain sacraments, there is no salvation without them; other sacraments are necessary for perfecting our salvation. Confirmation is necessary for salvation in the latter sense: one can be saved without it, so long as it is not omitted out of contempt for the sacrament.[1]

Not only can a person go to heaven without having received Confirmation, a person can go to heaven without having received the *grace* of Confirmation. But just because one can get to heaven without Confirmation does not mean that Confirmation has no effect on whether or not we will get there. As the Catechism reminds us:

---

[1] Aquinas, ST IIIa, q. 72, a. 1, ad 3 (Leonine 12:126).

The whole of man's history has been the story of dour combat with the powers of evil, stretching, so our Lord tells us, from the very dawn of history until the last day. Finding himself in the midst of the battlefield man has to struggle to do what is right, and it is at great cost to himself, and aided by God's grace, that he succeeds in achieving his own inner integrity [GS 37 § 2]. (CCC 409)

If we can only overcome the devil by grace, and if grace is given to us by the Holy Spirit, how much more so do we need the sacrament that endows us with the power of the Holy Spirit to help us contend victoriously.

For this reason, the Church desires that where possible, no one depart this life without Confirmation. In danger of death, any priest can confer the sacrament on any baptized person (CCC 1314). Even children who have not reached the age of discretion can and should be confirmed if they are in danger of death (CCC 1307; CIC, Canon 891).

The second consequence of Confirmation's being but a part of Christian Initiation is that, since in the Latin Rite Confirmation is not given with Baptism, it is the obligation of parents and pastors to make sure that children receive the sacrament at the appropriate time (CCC 1307; CIC, Canon 890). "Without Confirmation and Eucharist, Baptism is certainly valid and efficacious, but Christian initiation remains incomplete" (CCC 1306).

The third is that, since profiting from the graces offered to us through Confirmation requires that we be in a state of grace, and since children go a long time between their Baptism and their Confirmation, candidates for Confirmation should receive the Sacrament of Penance and Reconciliation prior to Confirmation in order to be sure that they are fit for the reception of the Holy Spirit (CCC 1310).

The fourth is that, since those who have not yet been confirmed have not yet been fully formed in the Christian faith, they should seek out sponsors, as their parents did for them in selecting godparents at their baptism; where possible it is recommended that these sponsors actually be one's baptismal godparents so as to emphasize the continuity of Christian Initiation (CCC 1311; CIC, Canons 892–893).

Outside of the central moment of Confirmation, the Church celebrates this sacrament with several signs and ceremonies that enrich the central moment and help us to celebrate it more reverently. These signs and symbols begin at the Chrism Mass on Holy Thursday. At that Mass, the bishop, as a successor of the Apostles who received the Holy Spirit on Pentecost, consecrates the chrism that will be used to anoint those who will be baptized and confirmed. For the baptized the chrism is a sign of their having received the Holy Spirit, and for those confirmed it is a sign of their being empowered by the Holy Spirit. No matter who actually confers the sacrament—the bishop or one of his priests—the sacrament has to be conferred with that chrism, just like prophets, priests, and kings were only anointed with holy oil in the Old Testament.

On the day of Confirmation, the signs and ceremonies of Confirmation continue from the signs and ceremonies of Baptism. Since Baptism is an indispensable prerequisite for Confirmation and since Confirmation follows Baptism in the Easter Vigil liturgy, the liturgy for Confirmation presupposes everything that happens in the liturgy of Baptism: the Sign of the Cross, the proclamation of the Word of God, the exorcisms, the renunciation of the devil, the sanctification of the water, the washing with water, the post-baptismal anointing, the donning of a white garment, and the lighting of the baptismal candle. Outside of the Easter Vigil, the liturgy for Confirmation draws an explicit connection with the liturgy for Baptism, beginning with the renewal of the baptismal promises (CCC 1298).

Following the renewal of the baptismal promises, the bishop prays over the candidates for Confirmation and asks the Holy Spirit to come down upon them, to help and guide them, and to endow them with the Gifts of the Holy Spirit (CCC 1299). There follows the central moment in which the bishop seals the candidate with the gift of that same Spirit by the sacramental anointing with chrism.

Effects of the Sacrament

Even though it may not be accompanied by the same visible signs as the first Pentecost and the first Confirmations, since Confirmation is our own personal pentecost, it effects a dramatic transformation of our lives. It does this by completing the grace of our Baptism, raising us to spiritual maturity, empowering us with mature spiritual responsibility, and imprinting a new sacramental character on our souls.

Confirmation completes our Baptism by conferring upon us a more complete sharing in the Holy Spirit. It is true that Baptism marks the entrance of the Holy Spirit into our souls. However, the presence of the Holy Spirit in our souls is not a simple yes-or-no question. The more we welcome the Holy Spirit into our souls, the more of an effect his presence will have on us. By participating in Confirmation, we cooperate with the grace of the Holy Spirit, which God wants to pour into our souls and open ourselves to a more complete reception of what was offered to us at Baptism: divine filiation, union with Christ, the Gifts of the Holy Spirit, and union with the Church (CCC 1302).

As mentioned above, the Gifts of the Holy Spirit have been associated with Confirmation in a particular way since Patristic times. Following the teaching of the Prophet Isaiah, the Church enumerates seven of these gifts: wisdom, understanding, counsel, fortitude, knowledge, piety, and fear of the Lord (Isa 11:1–2; CCC 1831). More than any other habitual graces that God gives us, these gifts make us act most like God because they give us a share in actions that belong first and foremost to God.[2]

Following the teaching of St. Paul, the Church also acknowledges twelve fruits that follow from a life lived in cooperation with these gifts: charity, joy, peace, patience, kindness, goodness, generosity, gentleness, faithfulness, modesty, self-control, and chastity (Gal 5:22–23; CCC 1832).

By completing our Baptism and conferring on us a special share in the gifts and fruits of the Holy Spirit, Confirmation raises us to the status of spiritual adults with adult responsibility in the Church. That does not mean that we automatically become natural adults or that Confirma-

---

[2] Aquinas, ST Ia–IIae, q. 68, a. 8, resp.

tion somehow changes our status in human society. A spiritual adult is someone who has received all the habitual grace proper to the mature Christian life and is thus called to an adult share of responsibility in the exercise of Christ's prophetic, priestly, and royal offices. This maturity and responsibility may or may not correlate with natural age. Sometimes very young children who receive the Sacrament of Confirmation early due to grave circumstances become powerful witnesses for Christ; other times adult converts who receive the sacrament without all the attention and preparation that it is due are lax in their public lives. What determines how well we will benefit from the graces given us at Confirmation is the level of interior cooperation that we give the Holy Spirit when it comes down upon us at Confirmation, not our external age.

If spiritual adulthood is not correlated with natural age, all the more so is Confirmation not correlated with a rite of passage into natural adulthood. As it happens, since in the Latin Rite the Church has set the age for Confirmation at the age of discretion, and since the age of discretion is the age at which people begin preparing to make adult decisions in their lives, Confirmation is often confused with one of those adult decisions that people make, like whether to get married or enter religious life, what college to go to, what career to choose, etc. People often treat Confirmation like it is the sacrament whereby *we* confirm what was professed on our behalf at our Baptism. But that is precisely the reverse of what happens. While we renew the promises made by us or on our behalf, it is *God* who confirms what was begun in us at Baptism. What began in us, moreover, was a free gift of God's grace—it does not need any further ratification to become effective (CCC 1308).

As a seal of all the graces that Confirmation imparts, it also imprints upon our souls a "character." That character, like the character of Baptism, gives us a share in Christ's prophetic, priestly, and royal offices. But it gives us a different share in those offices than the character of Baptism. St. Thomas Aquinas explains this well:

> Just as Baptism is a spiritual rebirth into the Christian life, so also is Confirmation a spiritual growing-up which brings a person into spiritual adulthood. Now, it is clear from a comparison with

bodily life that people who have just been born and those who arrive at adulthood do different sorts of things; therefore, by the Sacrament of Confirmation a person is given spiritual power for some more sacred actions beyond those for which that person is given power in Baptism. For in Baptism a person receives the power to do those things which pertain to his own salvation . . . but in Confirmation he receives the power to do those things which pertain to spiritual combat against enemies of the faith. This is clear from the example of the Apostles, who, before they had received the fullness of the Holy Spirit, were "in the upper room persevering in prayer" (see Acts 1:13–14); yet who, after they emerged, were not ashamed to confess their faith publicly, even in front of enemies of the Christian faith.[3]

Children lead more private lives because much of their energy is spent on their own physical, intellectual, and moral development. Even when they are with others—at school, for instance—they are often engaged in activities that have their own personal development as a goal. With adults it is otherwise. Although adults still need to develop intellectually and morally, they spend much more of their time in activities which have the development of others as their goal, be it raising a family, working to provide for a family, and/or undertaking some form of service. So also in the Christian life. By the character of Confirmation, Christians are empowered to take a public share in Christ's prophetic, priestly, and royal offices.

Appropriating and Living This Sacrament

Since Confirmation is our own personal Pentecost—the day on which the Holy Spirit is poured out upon us in all his power—the best way for us to appropriate and live this sacrament is to develop an ongoing relationship with the Holy Spirit. As with any relationship, we can do this in

---

[3] Aquinas, ST IIIa, q. 72, a. 5, resp. (Leonine 12:130).

three ways: by listening to the Holy Spirit, by meeting the Holy Spirit, and by spending time with the Holy Spirit. Through his Church, God provides us with ways of doing each of these things so that we may grow in an ever-deeper appreciation for and cooperation with the Holy Spirit's presence in our lives.

The first way in which we can develop a relationship with the Holy Spirit is by listening to the words that the Holy Spirit has spoken. The Church teaches that all the Sacred Scriptures "have been written down under the inspiration of the Holy Spirit," and that therefore, "they have God as their author and have been handed on as such to the Church herself" (CCC 105). For this reason, even though the different books of Sacred Scripture have many different human authors, they all have God as a common author (CCC 106). We can get to know the Holy Spirit by prayerfully reading the Sacred Scriptures in *lectio divina*; by praying in a way that draws us into the central mysteries in Sacred Scriptures, as in the Rosary; or praying some of the Liturgy of the Hours, which has the inspired prayers of the Psalms at its heart (CCC 1176, 2708).

The second way in which we can develop a relationship with the Holy Spirit is by meeting the Holy Spirit in the places he has invited us to meet him: the Church's liturgical celebrations and, above all, the sacraments. As mentioned previously, in each of the seven sacraments the Holy Spirit comes to us to bring grace into our souls; and while some sacraments, like Baptism, Confirmation, and Holy Orders, can only be received once because of the character that they imprint on our souls, other sacraments, like Reconciliation and Eucharist, can and should be received frequently (CCC 1389, 1458). Each time we participate in the sacraments worthily, we cooperate with the Holy Spirit, and his presence and grace grow in our souls.

The third way in which we can develop a relationship with the Holy Spirit is through prayer.

Every time we begin to pray to Jesus it is the Holy Spirit who draws us on the way of prayer by his prevenient grace. Since he teaches us to pray by recalling Christ, how could we not pray to the Spirit too? That is why the Church invites us to call upon the

Holy Spirit every day, especially at the beginning and the end of every important action. (CCC 2670)

Just as we can talk to Jesus because he is God, so likewise we can talk to the Holy Spirit. Even if we are having a hard time praying with words and simply offer our inward desires to God, St. Paul assures us that "the Spirit himself intercedes for us with sighs too deep for words" (Rom 8:26). The Church also gives us out of her tradition written prayers that we can say to the Holy Spirit. One such prayer is based upon the Sequence at Pentecost:

> Come, Holy Spirit, fill the hearts of your faithful and enkindle in them the fire of your love.
> V. Send forth your Spirit and they shall be created.
> R. And you shall renew the face of the earth.
> Let us pray. O God, who by the light of the Holy Spirit, did instruct the hearts of the faithful, grant us in the same Spirit to be truly wise and ever to rejoice in His consolation. Through Christ our Lord. Amen.[4]

However we pray, our relationship with the Holy Spirit helps us to embrace more thoroughly the call to grow from spiritual children to spiritual adults. We participate in Christ's royal office by going out into the world and bringing it under the reign of Christ; in Christ's priestly office by thereby consecrating the world to him through our prayers, good works, and apostolates; and in Christ's prophetic office by giving witness not just with our deeds but also with our words. Confirmation may not be associated with visible signs anymore like it was in the Acts of the Apostles, but perhaps that is because our public actions, which show the Holy Spirit at work in the world, are intended to take the place of those signs.

---

[4] This prayer is based on the sequence "Veni, Sancte Spiritus," found in the Lectionary, entry no. 63, http://www.usccb.org/bible/readings/052018-mass-during-day.cfm.

SELECTED READING
Thomas Aquinas, *Summa Theologiae* IIIa, q. 72, aa. 5–6[5]

Article 5. Whether the sacrament of Confirmation imprints a character?

Objection 1. It seems that the sacrament of Confirmation does not imprint a character. For a character means a distinctive sign. But a man is not distinguished from unbelievers by the sacrament of Confirmation, for this is the effect of Baptism; nor from the rest of the faithful, because this sacrament is ordained to the spiritual combat, which is enjoined to all the faithful. Therefore a character is not imprinted in this sacrament.

Objection 2. Further, it was stated above (III:63:2) that a character is a spiritual power. Now a power must be either active or passive. But the active power in the sacraments is conferred by the sacrament of order: while the passive or receptive power is conferred by the sacrament of Baptism. Therefore no character is imprinted by the sacrament of Confirmation.

Objection 3. Further, in circumcision, which is a character of the body, no spiritual character is imprinted. But in this sacrament a character is imprinted on the body, when the sign of the cross is signed with chrism on man's brow. Therefore a spiritual character is not imprinted by this sacrament.

On the contrary, A character is imprinted in every sacrament that is not repeated. But this sacrament is not repeated: for Gregory II says (Ep. iv ad Bonifac.): "As to the man who was confirmed a second time by a bishop, such a repetition must be forbidden." Therefore a character is imprinted in Confirmation.

---

[5] Reading Thomas Aquinas is a little bit different than reading other authors. He shapes what he says like a friendly argument. First he asks a question. Then he thinks of others first: "What objections might they have to what I want to say?" After he lists those objections, he responds to them with a short argument or quotation to show that reason and authority are on his side ("On the contrary . . ."). Then he says what he thinks ("I answer that . . ."). Then he carefully responds to each of the objections from others. St. Thomas does not frame things this way to be contentious. St. Paul warns us about that (1 Cor 1:10). Instead, St. Thomas frames things this way so that he and others together can clearly arrive at the truth.

I answer that, As stated above (III:63:2), a character is a spiritual power ordained to certain sacred actions. Now it has been said above (Article 1; III:65:1) that, just as Baptism is a spiritual regeneration unto Christian life, so also is Confirmation a certain spiritual growth bringing man to perfect spiritual age. But it is evident, from a comparison with the life of the body, that the action which is proper to man immediately after birth, is different from the action which is proper to him when he has come to perfect age. And therefore by the sacrament of Confirmation man is given a spiritual power in respect of sacred actions other than those in respect of which he receives power in Baptism. For in Baptism he receives power to do those things which pertain to his own salvation, forasmuch as he lives to himself: whereas in Confirmation he receives power to do those things which pertain to the spiritual combat with the enemies of the Faith. This is evident from the example of the apostles, who, before they received the fullness of the Holy Ghost, were in the "upper room . . . persevering . . . in prayer" (Acts 1:13-14); whereas afterwards they went out and feared not to confess their faith in public, even in the face of the enemies of the Christian Faith. And therefore it is evident that a character is imprinted in the sacrament of Confirmation.

Reply to Objection 1. All have to wage the spiritual combat with our invisible enemies. But to fight against visible foes, viz. against the persecutors of the Faith, by confessing Christ's name, belongs to the confirmed, who have already come spiritually to the age of virility, according to 1 John 2:14: "I write unto you, young men, because you are strong, and the word of God abideth in you, and you have overcome the wicked one." And therefore the character of Confirmation is a distinctive sign, not between unbelievers and believers, but between those who are grown up spiritually and those of whom it is written: "As new-born babes" (1 Peter 2:2).

Reply to Objection 2. All the sacraments are protestations of faith. Therefore just as he who is baptized receives the power of testifying to his faith by receiving the other sacraments; so he who is confirmed receives the power of publicly confessing his faith by words, as it were "ex officio."

Reply to Objection 3. The sacraments of the Old Law are called "justice of the flesh" (Hebrews 9:10) because, to wit, they wrought nothing inwardly. Consequently in circumcision a character was imprinted in the body only, but not in the soul. But in Confirmation, since it is a sacrament of the New Law, a spiritual character is imprinted at the same time, together with the bodily character.

Article 6. Whether the character of Confirmation presupposes of necessity, the baptismal character?

Objection 1. It seems that the character of Confirmation does not presuppose, of necessity, the baptismal character. For the sacrament of Confirmation is ordained to the public confession of the Faith of Christ. But many, even before Baptism, have publicly confessed the Faith of Christ by shedding their blood for the Faith. Therefore the character of Confirmation does not presuppose the baptismal character.

Objection 2. Further, it is not related of the apostles that they were baptized; especially, since it is written (John 4:2) that Christ "Himself did not baptize, but His disciples." Yet afterwards they were confirmed by the coming of the Holy Ghost. Therefore, in like manner, others can be confirmed before being baptized.

Objection 3. Further, it is written (Acts 10:44-48) that "while Peter was yet speaking . . . the Holy Ghost fell on all them that heard the word . . . and [Vulgate: for] they heard them speaking with tongues": and afterwards "he commanded them to be baptized." Therefore others with equal reason can be confirmed before being baptized.

On the contrary, Rabanus says (De Instit. Cleric. i): "Lastly the Paraclete is given to the baptized by the imposition of the high priest's hands, in order that the baptized may be strengthened by the Holy Ghost so as to publish his faith."

I answer that, The character of Confirmation, of necessity supposes the baptismal character: so that, in effect, if one who is not baptized were to be confirmed, he would receive nothing, but would have to be confirmed again after receiving Baptism. The reason of this is that, Confirmation is to Baptism as growth to birth, as is evident from what has been said above (Article 1; III:65:1). Now it is clear that no one can be brought to perfect age unless he be first born: and in like manner, unless a man be first baptized, he cannot receive the sacrament of Confirmation.

Reply to Objection 1. The Divine power is not confined to the sacraments. Hence man can receive spiritual strength to confess the Faith of Christ publicly, without receiving the sacrament of Confirmation: just as he can also receive remission of sins without Baptism. Yet, just as none receive the effect of Baptism without the desire of Baptism; so none receive the effect of Confirmation, without the desire of Confirmation. And man can have this even before receiving Baptism.

Reply to Objection 2. As Augustine says (Ep. cclxv), from our Lord's words, "'He that is washed, needeth not but to wash his feet' (John 13:10), we gather that Peter and Christ's other disciples had been baptized, either with John's Baptism, as some think; or with Christ's, which is more credible. For He did not refuse to administer Baptism, so as to have servants by whom to baptize others."

Reply to Objection 3. Those who heard the preaching of Peter received the effect of Confirmation miraculously: but not the sacrament of Confirmation. Now it has been stated (Reply to Objection 1) that the effect of Confirmation can be bestowed on man before Baptism, whereas the sacrament cannot. For just as the effect of Confirmation, which is spiritual strength, presupposes the effect of Baptism, which is justification, so the sacrament of Confirmation presupposes the sacrament of Baptism.

QUESTIONS FOR REVIEW

1. What are the essential words that must be spoken in the Sacrament of Confirmation?
2. Who is the original minister of Confirmation? Who else can administer this sacrament?
3. Is Confirmation necessary for salvation? Why or why not?

4. Name three effects of Confirmation.
5. What can affect the extent to which we benefit from the graces of Confirmation?

QUESTIONS FOR DISCUSSION

1. Do you remember your Confirmation? If so, what was special about the day? If not, or if you have not yet been confirmed, have you ever attended someone's Confirmation? What seemed interesting about that celebration?
2. Do you ever pray to the Holy Spirit? Why or why not? How could this help you grow stronger in your faith? How else could you strengthen your relationship with the Holy Spirit?

Part IV

The Eucharist

Holy Eucharist is the third of the seven sacraments, as well as the third Sacrament of Initiation. It is the greatest of the seven sacraments, the "source and summit of the Christian life" (CCC 1324). Its name comes from the Greek word *eucharistia*, meaning "thankfulness" or "gratitude." It also has a number of other names deriving from the various elements involved in its celebration and its effects: the Lord's Supper, the Breaking of Bread, the Eucharistic assembly, the Memorial of the Lord's Passion, the Holy Sacrifice of the Mass, the Holy and Divine Liturgy, and Holy Communion (CCC 1328–1331). All of these various names refer to one sacramental event:

> The eucharistic celebration is the action of Christ himself and the Church. In it, Christ the Lord, through the ministry of the priest, offers himself, substantially present under the species of bread and wine, to God the Father and gives himself as spiritual food to the faithful united with his offering. (CIC, Canon 899, §1)

In its central moment, when a priest says the words of Jesus over bread and wine (respectively: "This is my body" and "This is my blood"), those elements become the Body and Blood of Jesus and, through becoming his Body and Blood, are offered as a sacrifice to God—a re-presentation of the Sacrifice of Jesus on Calvary. They are given to the faithful to eat.

Chapter 1

UNDERSTANDING THE
SACRAMENT

Old Testament

‖ ASSIGNED READING
‖ Genesis 22:1–19
‖ Exodus 12

From the beginning of creation, sacrifice was the most basic form of the worship of God. When Cain and Abel, the children of Adam and Eve, wanted to give thanks to God, they offered sacrifices to God from what God had given them. Abel was a shepherd and he offered the firstlings of his flock; Cain was a farmer and offered some of his fruit (Gen 4:1–4). Although in some ancient cultures sacrifices were offered to appease supposedly angry gods, and people tried to find what the "right thing" was to sacrifice to make the gods happy (sometimes this even led to the abomination of child sacrifice), the Scriptures tell us that this was never the case with the God of Israel. God accepted Abel's sacrifice and rejected Cain's, but not because he had any preference for meat over fruit—"the LORD sees not as man sees; man looks on the outward appearance, but the LORD looks on the heart" (1 Sam 16:7). God looked at the heart of each man offering to see if his sacrifice was a sign of thankfulness to the

Lord. In Abel it was; in Cain it was not (Gen 4:4–7).

This pattern of sacrifice—offering some good thing back to God in thanksgiving for God's having given it to us—continued each time God performed some sort of saving action, especially those that prefigured Baptism and Confirmation. When Noah emerged safely from the Great Flood after encountering the dove, he "built an altar to the LORD, and took of every clean animal and of every clean bird, and offered burnt offerings on the altar" (Gen 8:20). When the Israelites emerged safely from the Red Sea following the pillar of cloud, God invited them to worship him with sacrifices in all the places where he came to them (Exod 20:24). When Jesus emerged from his baptism and the Holy Spirit alighted on him, he advanced deliberately over three years toward the sacrifice of himself on the Cross.

The fundamental element of any sacrifice was the offering of life. By purifying the people from sin with water and sending his Holy Spirit upon them—both in the Great Flood and in the Red Sea—God gave spiritual life back to a people who had lost it. Their sacrifices were a means of offering some portion of that life back to God. For this reason, all the animal sacrifices of the Old Testament followed a particular pattern: the Israelites would kill an animal, cook some or all of it, and, except in the case of a holocaust (a whole burnt offering), eat of its flesh. The one thing that they would never eat was the animal's blood, whether together with its body (in the form of raw flesh) or separate from its body. God explained why to Noah:

> Every moving thing that lives shall be food for you; and as I gave you the green plants, I give you everything. Only you shall not eat flesh with its life, that is, its blood. For your lifeblood I will surely require a reckoning; of every beast I will require it and of man; of every man's brother I will require the life of man. Whoever sheds the blood of man, by man shall his blood be shed; for God made man in his own image. (Gen 9:3–6)

The most important sacrifices in the Old Testament were those associated with covenants. When God promised Abraham land, children, and blessing, God asked two sacrifices of Abraham. The first was circumcision, whereby Abraham would offer back to God part of the means by which he would receive the blessing of children (Gen 17:9–14). The second was the sacrifice of his son, Isaac, which Abraham received as the firstfruits of that blessing (Gen 22). God did not actually allow Abraham to sacrifice his child. (Remember, child sacrifice is an abomination!) Rather, God demonstrated to Abraham through the event that there was nothing that Abraham could offer to God that was enough to establish himself in a covenant of kinship with God. You can only become a member of God's family if God himself raises you up by his grace. So, as Abraham remarked, "God will provide himself the lamb for a burnt offering" (Gen 22:8). And God did:

> Then Abraham put forth his hand, and took the knife to slay his son. But the angel of the LORD called to him from heaven, and said, "Abraham, Abraham!" And he said, "Here am I." He said, "Do not lay your hand on the lad or do anything to him; for now I know that you fear God, seeing you have not withheld your son, your only-begotten son, from me." And Abraham lifted up his eyes and looked, and behold, behind him was a ram, caught in a thicket by his horns; and Abraham went and took the ram, and offered it up as a burnt offering instead of his son. So Abraham called the name of that place The LORD will provide; as it is said to this day, "On the mount of the LORD it shall be provided." (Gen 22:10–14)

Sacrifices continued in the Mosaic Covenant. To prepare the Israelites to enter into a covenant with him as a nation, God saved them by means of another sacrifice, the sacrifice of the Paschal lamb (Exod 12:21–28; CCC 1334). God instructed the Israelites to kill this lamb and to paint the lintels of their doorposts with its blood. The blood of the Paschal lamb saved them from the angel of death that came through the land of Egypt and killed the firstborn of those who were oppressing God's people. When the Israelites were liberated from Egypt and brought to Mount Sinai to worship the Lord, they entered into a covenant with

God by a sacrifice in which they undertook the Law (Exod 24:1–8). Within the Mosaic Law, God made provision for a sacrificial priesthood that would offer daily sacrifices before the Lord (Exod 28–29).

Like all the signs and ceremonies of the Old Testament, the sacrifices of the Mosaic Law represented something that they could not make happen: the remembrance of God's having given the people spiritual life and the attempt to offer something of that life back to God in thanksgiving. The sacrifices were good in themselves, but they were not perfect. They could only feed a few people at a time; they could not make the past present again; they could represent the offering of a person's spiritual life to God, but they could not constitute it. Since these sacrifices did not *cause* anyone to be thankful to God, it was possible to participate in them with an unthankful or even evil heart—a possibility that God foresaw in Genesis, and one he condemns throughout the Old Testament in the starkest of terms:

> What to me is the multitude of your sacrifices?
>> says the LORD;
> I have had enough of burnt offerings of rams
>> and the fat of fed beasts;
> I do not delight in the blood of bulls,
>> or of lambs, or of he-goats.
> When you come to appear before me,
>> who requires of you
>> this trampling of my courts?
> Bring no more vain offerings; . . .
> Wash yourselves; make yourselves clean;
>> remove the evil of your doings
>> from before my eyes;
> cease to do evil,
>> learn to do good;
> seek justice,
>> correct oppression;
> defend the fatherless,
>> plead for the widow. (Isa 1:11–13, 16–17)

Already in the Old Testament, God foreshadowed the coming of a different sacrifice that would not be subject to the limitations of the Old Testament sacrifices.

- Where the sacrifices of the Mosaic Law could only feed a few, God foreshadowed a sacrifice that could feed the entirety of his people. He did this first through giving the Israelites manna in the wilderness (Exod 16:31–36; Num 11:1–14; Josh 5:10–12); he did it again by multiplying twenty loaves of barley and fresh ears of grain to feed a hundred men (2 Kings 4:42–44).

- Where the sacrifices of the Mosaic Law could only call to mind what God had done in the past, God foreshadowed a sacrifice in which his saving action would be continually present to his people. He did this first through the priest-king Melchizedek, who offered bread and wine (Gen 14:17–24; Heb 7:1–10) and who, being a priest outside the Mosaic Law, is said to have an everlasting priestly order (Ps 110:4). God did this again through the Bread of the Presence, which was prepared every Sabbath day and was to be set by the priests "before the LORD continually on behalf of the sons of Israel as a covenant for ever" (Lev 24:8).

- Where the sacrifices of the Mosaic Law *represented* the restoration of the Israelites to spiritual life, God foreshadowed a sacrifice in which the communication of that life would be achieved. He did this first through the Todah Sacrifice, the sacrifice of thanksgiving, in which bread and cakes were freely and graciously offered together with meat in gratuitous thanksgiving for God's intervention in one's life (Lev 7). He did it again through the prophecy of a suffering servant, who, like the sacrifices of old, would bear the sins of Israel upon his shoulders, but who, unlike those former sacrifices, would make righteous those who participated in his sacrifice (Isa 53:1–12).

New Testament

> ### ASSIGNED READING
> John 6
> Matthew 26:1–29
> Luke 22:1–23

Throughout his public ministry, Jesus indicated that he would fulfill the sacrificial expectations of the Old Testament by providing a miraculous food that would feed *all* of his people, would do so *continually*, and would do so in such a way as would *give* them spiritual life. He explains this most clearly in the Bread of Life Discourse in John 6.

In that discourse, Jesus first promises to feed all his people. He does this by showing them a sign of his ability to feed them miraculously. The sign is the Feeding of the Five Thousand (John 6:1–15; CCC 1335). People come to Jesus on the Passover, the feast on which the Israelites recalled being saved from sin by the blood of the lamb, without enough to eat. Jesus feeds them all miraculously by transforming five barley loaves and two fish into enough food to feed five thousand people. This miraculous provision is a sign of his ultimate intention: to provide miraculously for all his people true Passover food which will liberate them from sin.

After people see this miracle, they follow Jesus—not because they believe in him yet, or even because he did something more amazing than the prophets of old, but because they figured that they could get more food from Jesus (John 6:26). Jesus criticizes them for this; he reminds them that they should be seeking after the things of heaven, not the satisfaction of their bellies, and that to seek after the things of heaven, they should believe in him (John 6:27–29). Somehow not realizing that feeding five thousand people was a sign from God greater than the signs of old, the people ask Jesus to do something more; they remind him that Moses gave them manna to eat in the wilderness (John 6:30–31). Jesus, however, corrects them: it was not Moses who gave them manna; it was God, and since Jesus is God, he can give them all that they are seeking (John 6:33).

Second, Jesus promises to feed his people *forever*. He tells the people that he is the bread of life (John 6:35) and promises to those who accept what he says and believe in him that he will give them eternal life (John 6:40). But just like the people did not believe Jesus when he said he would feed them all, so likewise they don't believe him when he says he will feed them all forever. They "murmur" at him because they still do not understand (John 6:41; CCC 1336), which is the same thing that the Israelites had done when God gave them manna in the wilderness (Exod 17:3; Num 14:2). So, to remove any lack of clarity, Jesus specifies, "the bread which I shall give for the life of the world is my flesh" (John 6:51).

Third, Jesus promises to give his people spiritual *life*. The people did not understand this either. They did not understand how they could eat Jesus' flesh, let alone how eating his flesh could give them life. All of their sacrifices had involved eating the flesh of dead animals whose lives had already been offered to God by the shedding of their blood. Here Jesus does a new thing. He tells them that, unlike the sacrifices of the Old Testament in which the people were offering the life of an animal to God and so were forbidden from drinking its blood (remember, no take-backs), when Jesus sacrificed himself the people would eat his flesh *and drink his blood*, because God was offering his own life back to them (John 6:53–58).

At the Last Supper at the next Passover, on the night before Jesus offered himself once and for all as a sacrifice for the sins of humanity, Jesus fulfilled the promise he made at the previous Passover to give his disciples his flesh to eat and his blood to drink (CCC 1339–1340):

> Now as they were eating, Jesus took bread, and blessed, and broke it, and gave it to the disciples and said, "Take, eat; this is my body." And he took a chalice, and when he had given thanks he gave it to them, saying, "Drink of it, all of you; for this is my blood of the covenant, which is poured out for many for the forgiveness of sins. I tell you I shall not drink again of this fruit of the vine until that day when I drink it new with you in my Father's kingdom." (Matt 26:26–29; see CCC 1337)

There are several things that we must keep in mind if we are to understand the significance of what Jesus says here.

First, it is the anniversary of the Bread of Life Discourse; Jesus offers the Eucharist to his disciples a year after he promises to do so.

Second, it is the Passover. As such, it is a sacrificial meal, which calls to mind the sacrificial lamb by which God liberated his people and purified them from sin.

Third, we are at a particular point in the Passover meal. The ancient Passover meal involved four cups of wine.[1] The first began the ritual; the second recalled the Exodus; the third, the cup of blessing, concluded the main part of the meal and the celebration of what God had done; the fourth concluded the celebration. The cup that Jesus offered his disciples was the third cup, the cup of blessing; it was preceded by a blessing of unleavened bread, and by the consumption of the Paschal lamb.[2]

Fourth, by offering his disciples his body as the unleavened bread and his blood as the cup of blessing when they were about to eat the Paschal lamb, Jesus is telling his disciples that *he is the Paschal lamb* that they are about to eat, and that his *blood* is the blessing they are going to receive. Calling to mind what Jesus had said a year earlier, the disciples would have known precisely what they were going to do: they were going to eat the flesh of Jesus and drink his blood, which he offered miraculously to them all, so that they could receive life from him forever.

Fifth, when Jesus mentions drinking wine *again*, he is referring to the fourth cup, which concludes the Passover celebration. By saying that he will not drink it with them until they enter the Kingdom of the Father, Jesus is welcoming his disciples into a never-ending Passover, which will be celebrated in heaven.

Finally, as the Gospel of Luke and St. Paul record, Jesus commands his disciples to "Do this in remembrance of me" (Luke 22:19; 1 Cor 11:23–26; CCC 1342). As of old, when God instructed the Israelites to keep the Passover sacrifice in remembrance of his having liberated them from slavery to the Egyptians, now God commands his people to keep a

---

[1] Michael Barber, "The Mass and the Apocalypse," in *Scripture & The Mystery of the Mass* (Steubenville, OH: Emmaus Road, 2004), 127–141.

[2] For what follows, see Curtis Mitch, "The Mass and the Synoptic Gospels," in *Scripture & The Mystery of the Mass*, 23–36; Stephen Pimentel, "The Eucharist in the Apostolic Church," in *Scripture & The Mystery of the Mass*, 113–126.

new sacrifice in remembrance of Christ's liberating them from slavery to sin. This new sacrifice is to be kept in part after the pattern of the Todah, a continual thanksgiving for the saving work of God in which bread and wine are offered together with meat (CCC 1359–1361). The difference is that the bread and wine *become* meat—the flesh and blood of Jesus, the new Paschal lamb, by whose sacrifice God's people are freed from sin and restored to life. Rather than a *mere remembrance*, the Eucharist also *re-presents* the sacrifice of Jesus on the Cross (CCC 1341).

Since Jesus is God, when Jesus said, "This *is* my body" and "This *is* my blood," he made it happen that the bread and the wine became his Body and his Blood. Moreover, since Jesus commanded the Church to do likewise, when the Church speaks the words of Jesus, the same thing happens: the bread and wine become the Body and Blood of Jesus, and those who share in them become one with God and with one another because they are united with the Body of Jesus. If, as we said above, the Church is like a sacrament because it points out the union of people with God and with one another, the Eucharist is the means by which the Church is a sacrament. In a real sense, "the Church produces the Eucharist, but the Eucharist also produces the Church."[3] The disciples of Jesus make him sacrificially present, but it is only by partaking of his sacrificial presence that they fulfill the Greatest Commandments: to be united to him and to one another in love.

History and Theology

|| ASSIGNED READING
|| CCC 1322–1419

In the Patristic period, the reality revealed by the Scriptures was by and large taken for granted. Christ said that the Eucharist was his Body and Blood, and so it was. Christ offered it as a sacrifice, and so it was.

---

[3] Henri de Lubac, *The Splendor of the Church*, trans. Michael Mason (San Francisco: Ignatius Press, 1986), 133.

Concerning the change of the bread and wine into the Body and Blood of Jesus, Cyril of Jerusalem bears witness to the faith of the Fathers:

Even of itself the teaching of the Blessed Paul is sufficient to give you a full assurance concerning those Divine Mysteries, of which having been deemed worthy, you are become of the same body and blood with Christ. For you have just heard him say distinctly, "That our Lord Jesus Christ in the night in which He was betrayed, took bread, and when He had given thanks He broke it, and gave to His disciples, saying, Take, eat, this is My Body: and having taken the cup and given thanks, He said, Take, drink, this is My Blood" (1 Cor 11:23). Since then He Himself declared and said of the Bread, "This is My Body," who shall dare to doubt any longer? And since He has Himself affirmed and said, "This is My Blood," who shall ever hesitate, saying, that it is not His blood? . . .

Wherefore with full assurance let us partake as of the Body and Blood of Christ: for in the figure of Bread is given to you His Body, and in the figure of Wine His Blood; that you by partaking of the Body and Blood of Christ, may be made of the same body and the same blood with Him. For thus we come to bear Christ in us, because His Body and Blood are distributed through our members; thus it is that, according to the blessed Peter, we became "partakers of the divine nature" (2 Pet 1:4).[4]

Concerning the offering of the Body and Blood of Jesus, Augustine shows how the Church's understanding of the real presence of Jesus in the Eucharist, which unites us with him and with one another, can inform our understanding of the Eucharistic sacrifice.

Since, therefore, true sacrifices are works of mercy, which are referred to God, done either to ourselves or to our neighbors;

---

[4] Cyril of Jerusalem, *Mystagogical Catecheses* 4.1, 3 (NPNF 2.7:151).

but works of mercy are not done for any other reason but that we may be freed from misery and that thereby we may be happy (which only happens by way of that good, about which it is said: "it is good for me to cling to God"); it actually happens that this entire redeemed city, that is, the society of the saints gathered together, is offered as a universal sacrifice to God by its high priest, [Jesus,] who even sacrificed himself for us in his Passion, so that we might be the body of such a great head. . . . This is the sacrifice of Christians: "we, though many, are one body in Christ." The Church also celebrates this in the Sacrament of the Altar, known to the faithful, where it is shown to her that she herself is offered in the sacrifice which she offers.[5]

Transubstantiation

Jesus himself told us that the Eucharist was his Body and Blood, and that his Body and Blood was real food and real drink. But how is this possible? After all, the bread and wine of the Eucharist don't look like flesh and blood. They don't taste like flesh and blood. So, how are we supposed to understand the presence of Christ in the Eucharist?

The Church answers this question by telling us that the Body and Blood of Jesus are substantially present in the Eucharist. As St. Thomas Aquinas explained, that word "substance" can have a technical meaning. It means *what a thing is* beneath its appearance. In philosophy, "substance" is distinguished from "accidents." Accidents are *what can change about a substance* without changing what it is. You are a human being; that's your substance. But there are nine things that could change about you without changing you into something else. Those are your accidents:

1. How much of you there is (you could grow taller or lose weight; you're still you).
2. How you seem (you could seem happy or sad, energetic or sleepy; you're still you).

---

[5]   Augustine, *De civitate Dei* 10.6 (CSEL 40.1:456).

3. How you are related to others (you could get new brothers and sisters, nieces and nephews, or even get married; you're still you).

4. Where you are (you could go home, go to school, go to a friend's house; you're still you).

5. When you are (you're born one day, and with each passing day you're still you).

6. What position you're in (standing, sitting, or lying down, you're still you).

7. What you're wearing (whether a suit, a dress, or gym clothes, you're still you).

8. What you're doing (eating, sleeping, or doing religion homework, you're still you).

9. What's affecting you (whether you're hearing music or having your nails done, you're still you).

Ordinarily, as you go through life, you make judgments about the *substance* of things based on their *accidents*. If it is the size of a duck, it's in a row of ducks in a duck pond, it's covered in feathers, and it's quacking, then your mind tells you *it's a duck*. And 99% of the time when you make judgments like this, you're right. If it's the size of bread, the color of bread, with a bunch of other bread in a bread bowl at dinnertime waiting to be eaten, *it's bread*. What Jesus taught the disciples in the Gospel, and what the Church asks us all to believe, is that there is one exception to this rule: by the miraculous power of God, who gives to his priests the power to speak his words, it so happens that after the consecration at Mass, what looks, feels, smells, and tastes like bread is no longer bread; it is the Body of Jesus; what looks, feels, smells, and tastes like wine is no longer wine; it is the Blood of Jesus.

At the Fourth Lateran Council (1215), the Church taught that a good word to describe this miraculous change is "transubstantiation;"[6] the Church reiterated this teaching at the Council of Trent (1551).[7] "Trans-" means to pass from one thing to the next. Transubstantiation is

---

6 DH 802.
7 DH 1642.

when one substance, that of bread or wine, passes to the next, that of the Body and Blood of Jesus (CCC 1376). When the priest says, "this is my body" over the bread and, "this is my blood" over the wine, the Eucharistic elements still look, feel, smell, and taste like bread and wine; but they are the Body and Blood of Jesus (CCC 1374). Moreover, because the Body and Blood of Jesus are united to his Soul and his Divinity in heaven, these are present in the consecrated Eucharist as well (CCC 1413).

The Church believes in transubstantiation because the Church believes Jesus when he speaks simply and says, "this is my body" and "this is my blood." Just like it can't be raining and not raining at the same time, just like a shape cannot be a square and a circle at the same time, just like you can't be five feet tall and six feet tall at the same time, the Eucharist cannot be bread and wine as well as Jesus' Body and Blood at the same time. It's one or the other. And Jesus said it was his Body and Blood, not bread and wine (CCC 1375).

The Sacrifice of the Mass

Transubstantiation occurs in the context of the sacrifice of the Mass. This understanding—that the Mass is a sacrifice—is, in part, based on what Jesus says in Luke 22 during the Last Supper: "This chalice which is poured out for you is the new covenant in my blood" (v. 20).

As we have seen above, a covenant in the Old Testament was not just a promise; a covenant created a relationship that was sealed by an action. God sealed his covenant with Noah by making rainbows; God asked Abraham to seal his covenant with God by undergoing circumcision; God asked Moses to seal his covenant with God by performing animal sacrifices. It is no different in the New Testament. Jesus offers us a new covenant in his Blood. But he does not promise that we can benefit from that covenant without doing anything. The same Jesus who said, "the bread which I shall give for the life of the world is my flesh" (John 6:51) and, "unless you eat the flesh of the Son of man and drink his blood, you have no life in you" (John 6:53) also said that the chalice of his Blood in the Eucharist is "poured out" (Luke 22:20)—the same word that describes what Moses did to the oxen with which he ratified the Mosaic Covenant—and then commands his disciples to "Do this in remembrance of me" (1 Cor 11:24; CCC 1363–1365).

The Eucharist, therefore, is a covenantal sacrifice. Every time Mass is celebrated, our relationship with Jesus Christ, which was established by the new covenant in his Blood, is renewed through a re-presentation of Jesus' sacrifice. That sacrifice does not replace Jesus' sacrifice on the Cross; Jesus died once and for all for the sins of humanity. Rather, it renews Jesus' sacrifice on the Cross in an unbloody manner (CCC 1367). Every time Mass is said, the infinite merit that Jesus won upon the Cross for us is showered down upon the Church again, both for those alive and those who have died in Christ (CCC 1371).

The Eucharist does not end with the transubstantiation through which the Sacrifice of the Mass takes place, however. As we saw above, Jesus promised that his disciples would eat and drink of his sacrificial offering. Faithful to this teaching, the Church offers to the faithful the opportunity to eat of the sacrificial victim so that they may receive in their very bodies a share in his sacrifice. That sharing is called "Holy Communion" (CCC 1382–1384). Since the bread and wine are transubstantiated into the Body and Blood of Jesus at the Sacrifice of the Mass, when we receive Holy Communion the Body and Blood of Jesus are offered to us, together with his Soul and Divinity. The Church, wanting none of us to be separated from such an incredible gift, requires all the faithful to receive Holy Communion at least once per year, usually in the Easter season, and encourages us to receive it much more often—daily if possible (CCC 1388–1389).

QUESTIONS FOR REVIEW

1. What is the fundamental element of a sacrifice?
2. What could the sacrifices of the Old Testament not accomplish? What could they accomplish?
3. In what three ways did Jesus promise to fulfill the Old Testament sacrifices?
4. What is transubstantiation?
5. How is the Eucharist a sacrifice?

QUESTIONS FOR DISCUSSION

1. Have you ever made a sacrifice to God for yourself or for someone else? What kind of sacrifice did you make? Why did you make it?
2. Why do some people find it hard to believe that Jesus is truly present in the Eucharist? How can we explain transubstantiation in a way that makes sense to ordinary people?

Chapter 2

LIVING THE SACRAMENT

|| ASSIGNED READING
|| CIC, Canons 897–958

Celebration

Owing to the fact that Our Lord Jesus Christ himself comes to us bodily in the Eucharist and sacrifices himself for us, this sacrament is like no other. "The other sacraments, and indeed all ecclesiastical ministries and works of the apostolate, are bound up with the Eucharist and are oriented toward it. For in the blessed Eucharist is contained the whole spiritual good of the Church, namely Christ himself, our Pasch [PO 5]" (CCC 1324). For this reason, the celebration of this sacrament is more elaborate than that of any other sacrament.

There are six basic parts to the Mass:

1. **The Gathering**, in which the faithful are joined in worship together and prepared to enter into the Eucharistic sacrifice by a penitential rite.
2. **The Liturgy of the Word**, in which the Sacred Scriptures are read, then explained in a homily.
3. **The Offertory**, in which the bread and wine to be offered to God are prepared by the priest and other gifts of the people are brought forth.

4. **The Anaphora**, or "Offering," which is the central moment of the
    celebration. It includes:

    - *The Preface*, in which the Church thanks God for the things he
      has done over the course of Salvation History to prepare us to
      receive the sacrifice of Jesus.

    - *The Epiclesis*, in which the Church calls down the Holy Spirit
      on the bread and wine for the purpose of turning them into the
      Body and Blood of Jesus.

    - *The Institution Narrative*, in which the account of the Last Supper
      is recited and the Words of Institution are said. This is when
      transubstantiation and the Eucharistic sacrifice occur.

    - *The Anamnesis*, in which the Church recalls what God has done
      in the sacrifice of Jesus.

    - *The Intercessions*, in which the Church prays to Jesus who has
      been sacrificed for us.

5. **Communion**, in which the faithful receive Jesus, who has been
    sacrificed for us in the Eucharist.

6. **The Dismissal**, in which the faithful, having received Jesus, are
    blessed and sent out into the world to bring Jesus to it.

Each of the parts of Mass and each of the persons in the Mass are
essential to it. Unlike Baptism, in which all the ceremonial elements
except the central moment can be omitted in danger of death, and even
the central moment can be administered by anyone, the only minister
who can celebrate the Eucharist is a validly ordained priest (CCC 1411;
CIC, Canon 900, §1); and he can only celebrate the Eucharist with the
same materials that Jesus did: bread made from wheat and wine made
from grapes (CCC 1412; CIC, Canon 924). In the Latin Rite, following
ancient tradition, the bread must be unleavened as it was at the Passover
meals of the Israelites (CIC, Canon 926).

The Eucharist can never be consecrated outside of Mass no matter
how urgent the necessity may be, nor can the Words of Institution be
interrupted once they have started, even for the gravest of necessities
(CIC, Canon 927). It has been traditionally understood that even if a
priest were to die suddenly after consecrating the bread, another priest

would be required to continue the Mass and consecrate the wine so as to complete the sacrifice.[1] In cases of necessity, the Church permits other people to distribute Communion; these people are called "Extraordinary Ministers of Holy Communion," but they are not able to consecrate the Body and Blood of Jesus—they only distribute the Body and Blood of Jesus consecrated by the priest (CIC, Canon 230, §3; 910, §2).

Anyone can attend a Catholic Mass. But in order to receive Communion, it is necessary for a person to prepare himself or herself to be united with Jesus, so that what is signified on the outside—union with God and with one's neighbor—will match what happens on the inside. St. Paul tells us why:

> Whoever, therefore, eats the bread or drinks the cup of the Lord in an unworthy manner will be guilty of profaning the body and blood of the Lord. Let a man examine himself, and so eat of the bread and drink of the cup. For any one who eats and drinks without discerning the body eats and drinks judgment upon himself. That is why many of you are weak and ill, and some have died. But if we judged ourselves truly, we should not be judged. But when we are judged by the Lord, we are chastened so that we may not be condemned along with the world. (1 Cor 11:27–32)

In the Latin Rite, the Church has generally understood St. Paul to give two commands about the Eucharist here. When he speaks of "discerning the body" of Jesus, he means that people who are going to receive Communion should be baptized members of the Body of Christ, that is to say, the Church (CIC, Canon 912); should have attained the age of reason; and should believe that the bread and wine in the Eucharist are transubstantiated into the Body and Blood of Jesus (CIC, Canon 913, §1). When he speaks of "judging ourselves truly," he means that we should examine our consciences before receiving the Eucharist to make

---

[1] Council of Trent, Decree on Defects that May Occur in the Celebration of Mass *De defectibus*, 33.

sure that we have not committed any mortal sins that have not already been forgiven either through Baptism, or after Baptism through the Sacrament of Penance and Reconciliation (CCC 1385; CIC, Canons 915–916). The reason for this is simple: if we are in a state of grace, we are united to Jesus primarily as our merciful Savior, who increases in us the grace we have already received from him (CCC 1391); if we are not in a state of grace, we are united to him primarily as our just Judge, from whom we cannot hide the faults that separate us from him.

Provided that we are in a state of grace, the Church asks one more thing of us: that we fast before receiving Communion. Again, St. Paul tells us why:

> But in the following instructions I do not commend you, because when you come together it is not for the better but for the worse. For, in the first place, when you assemble as a Church, I hear that there are divisions among you; and I partly believe it, for there must be factions among you in order that those who are genuine among you may be recognized. When you meet together, it is not the Lord's supper that you eat. For in eating, each one goes ahead with his own meal, and one is hungry and another is drunk. What! Do you not have houses to eat and drink in? Or do you despise the Church of God and humiliate those who have nothing? What shall I say to you? Shall I commend you in this? No, I will not. (1 Cor 11:17–22)

If we don't fast before receiving Communion, then we do nothing to take our minds off of ordinary food and turn them toward receiving Jesus; we may also cause scandal to our neighbors, who may not have as much food as we do. So, in order for our Communion to be an occasion to love God and to love our neighbor, the Church requires that we fast from everything but water and medicine for one hour before receiving Communion (CIC, Canon 919, §1).

If we are baptized members of the Catholic Church, we are not conscious of having committed any grave sins since our last sacramental Confession, and we have fasted for one hour, then not only *can* we receive Communion, we *should* (CCC 1388; CIC, Canon 918). Jesus and his Church want us to receive Communion because Jesus wants us to love him and to love our neighbor, and he has given us the Eucharist through his Church as the best means of doing so. Jesus awaits us at every Mass. The only restriction on the reception of Communion to those who are eligible and properly prepared is that if you have already received Communion on a given day you can only receive Communion one more time that day, and then only if you are participating in the Eucharistic celebration (CIC, Canon 917).

While nothing can dispense a person from the obligation to be free of mortal sin to receive Communion, the requirement to fast before receiving the Eucharist and the limit on receiving it two times per day are dispensed if a person is in danger of death. In this case, the Church offers the Eucharist to the dying person as *Viaticum*, which is a Latin word meaning "food for the journey" to meet Jesus (CCC 1525). Jesus and his Church earnestly desire that every person depart this life as close to Jesus as possible. Thus, even outside of Mass, Communion is offered to the dying who have already received the Eucharist that day, and the Church urges them to receive it early so that they can participate in it fully, actively, and consciously (CIC, Canon 921).

Although persons outside of a state of grace or who lack proper preparation are physically capable of taking the Body and Blood of Jesus from a priest and consuming it, this should never be done. Since Jesus' priests transubstantiate bread and wine into his Body and Blood, people who are not in a state of grace or who lack proper preparation really do receive the Body and Blood of Jesus, but as St. Paul says, they "eat and drink judgment upon themselves" by committing the sin of sacrilege (CCC 2120).

Effects of the Sacrament

Wherever the Holy Spirit dwells, it calls for the Lord Jesus; since the Holy Spirit has been poured out upon the Church, the Church calls for the Lord Jesus; and when through Baptism and Confirmation the

Church pours out the Holy Spirit upon us, we should call for the Lord Jesus as well.

> The Spirit and the Bride say, "Come." And let him who hears say, "Come." And let him who is thirsty come, let him who desires take the water of life without price. (Rev 22:17)

What the Church and her members yearn for is the Second Coming of Jesus, when Jesus "will come in the same way as [the disciples] saw him go into heaven" (Acts 1:11). At that time the mission of the Church will be fulfilled: to bring all the world into the kingdom of Christ (CCC 671–672). In the meantime, since we do not know when Jesus will come again (CCC 673), we are left with the Eucharist as the closest means of approaching him in this life and as our anticipation of a yet more glorious sharing in his life in the world to come (CCC 1402–1404).

Even if our union with Jesus through the Eucharist is not the final union for which the Holy Spirit yearns in our hearts, it nevertheless brings us into a complete sharing of the Christian life on earth. For that reason, the reception of the Eucharist is the completion and fulfillment of Christian Initiation. A person who has received Baptism, Confirmation, and the Eucharist has already lived out the entire pattern of the Christian life: welcoming the Holy Spirit into their heart, strengthening the Holy Spirit in their heart, and following the Holy Spirit to union with Jesus, as well as with all the other people who have been united with him in his Body, the Church (CCC 1391, 1396).

As the fulfillment of Christian Initiation, the Eucharist is also the fulfillment of the Greatest Commandments of Jesus: to love God and to love our neighbor. Every time we receive the Eucharist with proper preparation, our union with Jesus pours charity into our hearts (CCC 1393). By increasing in our hearts what sin weakens, this charity brings with it the forgiveness of all our venial sins and preserves us from committing any future mortal sins (CCC 1394–1395). Our union with God, who humbled himself to die for us (Phil 2:1–10), also commits us to union with the poor, who are humbled by their state (CCC 1397). Seeing Jesus in the Eucharist helps us see Jesus in them (CCC 2449).

Precisely insofar as the Eucharist completes our Baptism by uniting us with Christ, making us part of his Body, it also reminds us of those who have been baptized, and so who are Christians, but who do not share in that complete unity with Christ in his Body. This reminder is painful; it brings to our remembrance all the past sins by which that unity was broken and our present failure to heal them completely (CCC 817). For this reason, Holy Communion challenges us to pray fervently for the full ecclesial unity of all those who have been baptized (CCC 1398). Such prayers for Christian unity are good, holy, and necessary (CCC 820–821). However, Catholics must be careful not to share in the Eucharist with other Christians who are not yet in full communion with the Catholic Church.

Since the Eucharist is a sign of union with God and with our neighbor, if we shared the Eucharist with someone with whom we were not in ecclesial unity, our Communion would be a sign of something that was not true—we would in fact be lying (CIC, Canons 844, §1; 908). Only in cases of true necessity, where it is physically or morally impossible to approach a Catholic priest, may a Catholic receive the Eucharist from a non-Catholic; and in that case, it must be from a priest who truly possesses the Sacrament of Holy Orders and so can truly offer the Eucharist, such as an Eastern Orthodox priest (CCC 1400; CIC, Canon 844, §§2–3). Protestant denominations do not possess the Sacrament of Holy Orders and so are not able to perform transubstantiation and the Sacrifice of the Mass; consequently, they cannot offer Catholics the Eucharist even in cases of grave necessity (CCC 1399). What they celebrate as "Eucharist" is not transubstantiated into the Body and Blood of Jesus; they call it by the same name, but it is not the same thing.

Appropriating and Living This Sacrament

Since the Eucharist given to us at Mass is the source and summit of the Christian life, there is no better way to appropriate and live this sacrament than by a "full, conscious, and active participation" in the celebration of the Mass (CCC 1141). The key to this participation is the contemplation of the sacrificial character of the Mass.[2] At Mass, the ordained priest—and he alone—offers the Eucharistic Prayer in which the Words of Institution are said, the bread and wine are transubstantiated into the Body and Blood of Jesus, and the Eucharistic sacrifice occurs.[3] Nevertheless, since by the Holy Spirit the Church has been united with Christ as his body,

> *the Eucharist is also the sacrifice of the Church.* The Church which is the Body of Christ participates in the offering of her Head. With him, she herself is offered whole and entire. She unites herself to his intercession with the Father for all men. In the Eucharist the sacrifice of Christ becomes also the sacrifice of the members of his Body. The lives of the faithful, their praise, sufferings, prayer, and work, are united with those of Christ and with his total offering, and so acquire a new value. Christ's sacrifice present on the altar makes it possible for all generations of Christians to be united with his offering. (CCC 1368)

As members of the Church, we participate fully, consciously, and actively at Mass when we pay attention to the celebration of Mass and unite ourselves, our desires, and our daily lives with the offering of Jesus by the Church. We do this first of all through reverent attention to the Mass as it unfolds. Such inward attention includes our vocal participation in those parts of the Mass assigned to the lay faithful: "acclamations, responses, psalmody, antiphons, and songs, as well as . . . actions, gestures, and bodily attitudes" that are prescribed by the Church, together with periods of silent prayer.[4] Where appropriate, it may also include participation in a genuine liturgical function, such as "servers, readers, commentators, and members of the choir" (CCC 1143).

The fruit of a full, conscious, and active participation at Mass is a

---

[2] Congregation for Divine Worship and the Discipline of the Sacrament, Instruction on Certain Matters to Be Observed or to Be Avoided Regarding the Most Holy Eucharist *Redemptionis Sacramentum* (March 25, 2004), §38.

[3] Congregation for Divine Worship and the Discipline of the Sacrament, *Redemptionis Sacramentum*, §52.

[4] Second Vatican Council, Dogmatic Constitution on the Church *Sacrosanctum Concilium* (December 4, 1963), §30.

life of charity centered on the union with God and our neighbor that we receive in Holy Communion; it is a life centered on and informed by the Mass; it is a life in which we spend the time before Mass preparing our hearts through prayer and, when necessary, sacramental Confession, and in which we spend the time after Mass giving thanks to God in our words and in our actions for giving us his Body and Blood (CCC 1358–1359). In order to help us lead a Mass-centered life, the Church recommends to us a variety of pious practices that help us call more deeply for Jesus to come to us in the Eucharist now and at his Second Coming hereafter.

The first of these practices is that of giving thanks immediately after receiving Jesus in Holy Communion. The entire Church observes this practice at Mass with a period of silence after the reception of Holy Communion.[5] But in most places the faithful can be found even after Mass spending some extra time in prayer and thanksgiving to Jesus for coming to them in Holy Communion. These extra moments in prayer and thanksgiving after Mass can help us build a habit of prayerfulness and attention to the presence of Jesus in our hearts throughout the day.

The second of these practices is that of showing worship to Jesus in the Eucharist outside of Mass. Since the Eucharist not only *points* to Jesus but actually *is* Jesus, there is nothing wrong with giving it the same worship that we give to Jesus; in fact, the worship of the Eucharist is an integral part of growing closer to Jesus. For that reason, every Catholic Church has a tabernacle or monstrance where the Eucharist is reserved for prayer and adoration (CCC 1379; CIC, Canon 934, §1), and it is customary to genuflect while making the Sign of the Cross when passing before it. Some people make a habit of weekly "Holy Hours," in which they spend one hour per week adoring Jesus in the Eucharist; but any visit to Jesus in the Eucharist can increase our love for him and for our neighbor, even if we just stop by Church for a brief moment, as we would to say hello to our neighbor.[6]

---

[5] *The Roman Missal*, trans. The International Commission on English in the Liturgy, 3rd typical ed. (Washington, DC: United States Conference of Catholic Bishops, 2011), §§138–139.

[6] Congregation for Divine Worship and the Discipline of the Sacrament, *Redemptionis Sacramentum*, §135.

SELECTED READING
John Paul II, Encyclical Letter on the Eucharist in Its
Relationship to the Church *Ecclesia de Eucharistia*, nos.
22–25

Incorporation into Christ, which is brought about by Baptism, is
constantly renewed and consolidated by sharing in the Eucharistic
Sacrifice, especially by that full sharing which takes place in sacramental communion. We can say not only that *each of us receives
Christ*, but also that *Christ receives each of us.* He enters into friendship with us: "You are my friends" (*Jn* 15:14). Indeed, it is because
of him that we have life: "He who eats me will live because of me"
(*Jn* 6:57). Eucharistic communion brings about in a sublime way the
mutual "abiding" of Christ and each of his followers: "Abide in me,
and I in you" (*Jn* 15:4).

By its union with Christ, the People of the New Covenant, far
from closing in upon itself, becomes a "sacrament" for humanity, a
sign and instrument of the salvation achieved by Christ, the light of
the world and the salt of the earth (cf. *Mt* 5:13-16), for the redemption of all. The Church's mission stands in continuity with the
mission of Christ: "As the Father has sent me, even so I send you" (*Jn*
20:21). From the perpetuation of the sacrifice of the Cross and her
communion with the body and blood of Christ in the Eucharist, the
Church draws the spiritual power needed to carry out her mission.
The Eucharist thus appears as both *the source* and *the summit* of all
evangelization, since its goal is the communion of mankind with
Christ and in him with the Father and the Holy Spirit.

Eucharistic communion also confirms the Church in her unity
as the body of Christ. Saint Paul refers to this *unifying power* of participation in the banquet of the Eucharist when he writes to the Corinthians: "The bread which we break, is it not a communion in the
body of Christ? Because there is one bread, we who are many are one
body, for we all partake of the one bread" (*1 Cor* 10:16-17). Saint
John Chrysostom's commentary on these words is profound and
perceptive: "For what is the bread? It is the body of Christ. And what

do those who receive it become? The Body of Christ—not many bodies but one body. For as bread is completely one, though made of up many grains of wheat, and these, albeit unseen, remain nonetheless present, in such a way that their difference is not apparent since they have been made a perfect whole, so too are we mutually joined to one another and together united with Christ." The argument is compelling: our union with Christ, which is a gift and grace for each of us, makes it possible for us, in him, to share in the unity of his body which is the Church. The Eucharist reinforces the incorporation into Christ which took place in Baptism though the gift of the Spirit (cf. *1 Cor* 12:13, 27).

The joint and inseparable activity of the Son and of the Holy Spirit, which is at the origin of the Church, of her consolidation and her continued life, is at work in the Eucharist. This was clearly evident to the author of the *Liturgy of Saint James*: in the epiclesis of the Anaphora, God the Father is asked to send the Holy Spirit upon the faithful and upon the offerings, so that the body and blood of Christ "may be a help to all those who partake of it . . . for the sanctification of their souls and bodies." The Church is fortified by the divine Paraclete through the sanctification of the faithful in the Eucharist.

The gift of Christ and his Spirit which we receive in Eucharistic communion superabundantly fulfils the yearning for fraternal unity deeply rooted in the human heart; at the same time it elevates the experience of fraternity already present in our common sharing at the same Eucharistic table to a degree which far surpasses that of the simple human experience of sharing a meal. Through her communion with the body of Christ the Church comes to be ever more profoundly "in Christ in the nature of a sacrament, that is, a sign and instrument of intimate unity with God and of the unity of the whole human race."

The seeds of disunity, which daily experience shows to be so deeply rooted in humanity as a result of sin, are countered by *the unifying power* of the body of Christ. The Eucharist, precisely by building up the Church, creates human community.

The *worship of the Eucharist outside of the Mass* is of inestimable value for the life of the Church. This worship is strictly linked to the celebration of the Eucharistic Sacrifice. The presence of Christ under the sacred species reserved after Mass—a presence which lasts as long as the species of bread and of wine remain—derives from the celebration of the sacrifice and is directed towards communion, both sacramental and spiritual. It is the responsibility of Pastors to encourage, also by their personal witness, the practice of Eucharistic adoration, and exposition of the Blessed Sacrament in particular, as well as prayer of adoration before Christ present under the Eucharistic species.

It is pleasant to spend time with him, to lie close to his breast like the Beloved Disciple (cf. *Jn* 13:25) and to feel the infinite love present in his heart. If in our time Christians must be distinguished above all by the "art of prayer," how can we not feel a renewed need to spend time in spiritual converse, in silent adoration, in heartfelt love before Christ present in the Most Holy Sacrament? How often, dear brother and sisters, have I experienced this, and drawn from it strength, consolation and support!

This practice, repeatedly praised and recommended by the Magisterium, is supported by the example of many saints. Particularly outstanding in this regard was Saint Alphonsus Liguori, who wrote: "Of all devotions, that of adoring Jesus in the Blessed Sacrament is the greatest after the sacraments, the one dearest to God and the one most helpful to us." The Eucharist is a priceless treasure: by not only celebrating it but also by praying before it outside of Mass we are enabled to make contact with the very wellspring of grace. A Christian community desirous of contemplating the face of Christ in the spirit which I proposed in the Apostolic Letters *Novo Millennio Ineunte* and *Rosarium Virginis Mariae* cannot fail also to develop this aspect of Eucharistic worship, which prolongs and increases the fruits of our communion in the body and blood of the Lord.

QUESTIONS FOR REVIEW

1. What are the six basic parts of the Mass?
2. Can the Eucharist ever be consecrated outside of the Mass?
3. Who can and cannot receive Communion? Why?
4. What commandments of Christ does the Eucharist fulfill?
5. What are the effects in our soul of receiving the Eucharist?

QUESTIONS FOR DISCUSSION

1. What is the best thing you remember about your First Holy Communion? If you have not already received First Holy Communion, have you ever been to someone else's First Holy Communion? Why did people make such a big deal out of that day?
2. Have you ever spent time with Jesus in the Eucharist outside of Sunday Mass? If so, describe. What did you do? What was it like? How did it help you? Is there any way you could make this a regular habit? If not, how do you think that doing so might change you?

Part V

PENANCE AND RECONCILIATION

An old saying among theologians has it that "grace is the seed of glory." When the life of grace takes root in our souls through Baptism, when it is strengthened through Confirmation, and when it is nourished by the Eucharist, it develops organically into the life of glory in heaven, where we will enjoy the vision of God with the saints for all eternity. All we have to do is not let anything get in the way.

The only thing that can get in the way of grace and glory is sin. Sin tarnishes the life of grace in our souls. If it is venial, it wounds charity and so reduces the degree of glory for which we are bound; if it is mortal, it destroys charity by excluding the Holy Spirit from our souls altogether.

God is remarkably consistent in his response to sin. Just as he did not leave the human race unaided when Adam and Eve sinned but, instead, promised us a redeemer, and just as he did not leave us in the dark about our redemption but gave us sacraments through which we could know we were receiving it, so neither does God leave us unaided if, after Baptism, Confirmation, and/or the Eucharist, we fall from grace by sin.

Baptism is for us a first forgiveness of our sins. But if we should sin after Baptism once, or seven times, or seventy times seven or more, God still extends his merciful hand toward us (Matt 18:21). He does not do this through baptizing us again, however. Once we have received the character of Baptism, we possess forever the indelible mark of Christ on our souls and have no need to receive it again. Instead, we need the grace corresponding with that mark to be restored. It is for this purpose that Jesus instituted the Sacraments of Healing (CCC 1420–1421). These two sacraments, the Sacrament of Penance and Reconciliation, and the Sacrament of Anointing of the Sick, restore us to grace and perfect us for glory so that no matter how many times we may fall, we may yet attain to the fullness of glory for which our Baptism, our Confirmation, and our worthy receptions of Holy Communion have prepared us.

The Sacrament of Penance and Reconciliation is the fourth of the seven sacraments and the first Sacrament of Healing. Over the course of the centuries, it has been known by a variety of names: the Sacrament of Penance, the Sacrament of Confession, the Sacrament of Reconciliation, the Sacrament of Conversion, and the Sacrament of Forgiveness (CCC 1423–1424). All of these names point to the same reality:

> In the sacrament of penance the faithful who confess their sins to a legitimate minister, are sorry for them, and intend to reform themselves obtain from God through the absolution imparted by the same minister forgiveness for the sins they have committed after baptism and, at the same time, are reconciled with the Church which they have wounded by sinning. (CIC, Canon 959)

The result of a good Confession is a "spiritual resurrection," in which we are once again raised up into friendship and fellowship with God (CCC 1468).

Chapter 1

UNDERSTANDING THE SACRAMENT

Old Testament

When we spoke about Baptism, we examined the crucial points in the history of the people of Israel when God cleansed the people from sin *en masse*: the Great Flood and the Crossing of the Red Sea. These cleansings prefigured Baptism, in which God washes away our sins *en masse* and gives us his Holy Spirit. But in addition to these cleansings there were also particular instances in which a notable person who was already in a relationship with God committed some particular sin and needed to be forgiven for that particular sin. Each of these instances followed a similar pattern: the person sinned; God confronted them; when or if they made a sincere confession to God, God forgave them.

The first instance of this is the first sin, that of Adam and Eve. God had given Adam and Eve a very particular commandment not to eat of the fruit of the Tree of the Knowledge of Good and Evil; if they did, he imposed a penalty: "in the day that you eat of it you shall die" (Gen 2:17). Of course Adam and Eve did eat that fruit, and while they did not die physically in that moment, they did die spiritually because their souls were separated from God. In full knowledge of what they had done, God confronts them: "Have you eaten of the tree of which I commanded you not to eat?" (Gen 3:11).

It is not as though God did not know what they had done. God is omniscient; he knows all things.[1] Rather, like a parent who knows that his or her child has broken the rules but wants to give the child a chance to acknowledge what he or she has done, God gives Adam and Eve a chance to confess their sin to him. Each of them hesitates but then confesses. Adam blames Eve, but then confesses, "I ate" (Gen 3:12). Eve blames the serpent, but then confesses, "I ate" (Gen 3:13).

God, for his part, imposes an appropriate punishment on Adam and Eve; he expels them from the Garden lest they eat of the Tree of Life and live forever apart from God (Gen 3:22). It's not that God has a problem with Adam and Eve living forever—he had given them the fruit of the Tree of Life for that very purpose—it is just that God wanted them to live forever *with him*; and so, even though he expels them from the Garden, he does not cast them away from his presence. In his boundless mercy, God offers them the forgiveness of their sins through the promise of a redeemer (Gen 3:15) and the mitigation of the consequences of their sin by giving them garments of skins (Gen 3:21), something much more suitable than fig leaves for life outside of Paradise!

Since Adam and Eve confess their sin to God, they are restored to a relationship with God even though they must now suffer the consequences of their sin. It is not so with their son, Cain. Out of envy for Abel's righteousness, Cain kills his brother Abel in a field (Gen 4:8). God gives Cain an opportunity to confess his sin by asking Cain the same sort of question he asked Adam and Eve: "Where is Abel your brother?" Unfortunately, Cain does not fess up. Unlike Adam and Eve, who hesitate but ultimately confess their sin, Cain lies and talks back to the Lord: "I do not know; am I my brother's keeper?" (Gen 4:9). The Lord is not so

---

[1] Aquinas, ST Ia, q. 14, a. 1.

easily fooled. "What have you done? The voice of your brother's blood is crying to me from the ground" (Gen 4:10).

As with Adam and Eve, God imposes a punishment on Cain for his sin (Gen 4:12); God even lightens that punishment out of mercy when Cain complains about it (Gen 4:13–15). But there are two things missing from the story of Cain: first, Cain never does confess his sin to God the way that Adam and Eve do; second, God never therefore promises Cain the forgiveness of his sin. Much to the contrary! The story of Cain ends with one of the most chilling phrases in all of Holy Scripture: "Then Cain went away from the presence of the Lord" (Gen 4:16); the Scriptures never tell us that he returned.

Already in these first two stories of the first two sins, we can discern a certain pattern at work in humanity's relationship with God. When we commit a serious sin, we die a spiritual death by losing the presence of the Holy Spirit in our souls. In order to be reconciled to God and receive the Holy Spirit again, God asks us to confess our sins to him. If we do so sincerely, he is ready to forgive our sins and has promised us forgiveness, but the forgiveness of our sins is not free of all consequence: God gives us some fitting consequences by which we are healed from the effects of our sin and taught not to sin again. On the other hand, if we refuse to confess our sin, we are not reconciled to God. Indeed, we "go away from the presence of the Lord" with Cain.

This pattern reoccurs often throughout the Old Testament. When God commands King Saul to destroy the Amalekites, including their sheep and cattle, but Saul captures the King of the Amalekites and helps himself to the spoils of war, God sends the prophet Samuel to question Saul and to give him an opportunity to repent. Saul initially lies, just like Cain: "Blessed be you to the LORD; I have performed the commandment of the LORD" (1 Sam 15:13). But the Lord is not so easily fooled. "What then is this bleating of the sheep in my ears, and the lowing of the oxen which I hear?" (1 Sam 15:14). God knows exactly what Saul has done (1 Sam 15:16, 19), and so he imposes a penalty on Saul just as he imposed a penalty on Cain: Saul does not get to be king anymore. "Because you have rejected the word of the LORD, he has also rejected you from being king" (1 Sam 15:23).

Here is where things get interesting. Unlike Cain, Saul sees his punishment as an opportunity to repent. He says to Samuel: "I have sinned; for I have transgressed the commandment of the LORD and your words, because I feared the people and obeyed their voice. Now therefore, I beg, pardon my sin, and return with me, that I may worship the LORD" (1 Sam 15:24–25). Yet, although Saul says all the words on the outside associated with repentance, he does not really repent on the inside. Saul is not sorry that he did anything wrong; Saul only says he is sorry because he is hoping to get out of his punishment. But the Lord sees right through it. Samuel rebukes Saul again (1 Sam 15:26), and only when Saul is truly sorry for his sin and accepts the consequences of his sin does Samuel accept Saul's apology. Only when Saul wants to make up for what he has done is he allowed once again to go with Samuel to worship the Lord (1 Sam 15:30–31).

In addition, therefore, to the confession of sins having an outward component in the Old Testament, it also has an inward component. When people sin, they must confess their sins to God. But the confession of their lips must be matched by inward sincerity: true sorrow for what they have done, faithful acceptance of the consequences, and a firm desire not to do it again.

Throughout the course of the Old Testament, God reserved the forgiveness of sins to himself, but he did call people to help others understand *when* he had forgiven sins. Sometimes he called them to a prophetic ministry and gave them the authority to pronounce his forgiveness. We have already seen that the prophet Samuel performed this role for Saul. Similarly, the prophet Nathan performed this role for King David (2 Sam 12:1–23) and the prophetess Huldah performed it for King Josiah (2 Kings 22:14–20).

Other times, God called people to a priestly ministry and gave them the authority to perform signs that represented the forgiveness that people *would* receive *if* they sincerely repented from their sins. Chief among these signs was the yearly liturgy on the Day of Atonement (Lev 16). That day was the one day during the year on which Aaron and his successors, the high priests, went into the inner sanctuary and made an atoning sacrifice for the sins of the people of Israel. First Aaron made a sin offering for himself of a bull and a sin offering for the people of a goat, and he sprinkled the blood of those offerings all over the inner sanctuary; then he took a live goat:

> And when he has made an end of atoning for the holy place and the tent of meeting and the altar, he shall present the live goat; and Aaron shall lay both his hands upon the head of the live goat, and confess over him all the iniquities of the sons of Israel, and all their transgressions, all their sins; and he shall put them upon the head of the goat, and send him away into the wilderness by the hand of a man who is in readiness. The goat shall bear all their iniquities upon him to a solitary land; and he shall let the goat go in the wilderness. (Lev 16:20–22)

The liturgy of atonement, including the scapegoat, represented the repentance of the people of Israel from their sins. However, let us recall that in the Old Testament there were no sacraments properly speaking; the scapegoat was a sign of the sins of the Israelites being sent away, but it was not also a *cause* of their sins being sent away. There was nothing about the liturgy of atonement that actually *made* the Israelites repent from their sins (Heb 9:9); it was perfectly possible to attend the ceremonies outwardly and appear to be repentant, but to cling to one's sins on the inside like Saul.

New Testament

|| ASSIGNED READING
|| Matthew 18:1–22
|| Luke 7:36–50

In the New Testament, Jesus fulfilled both the prophetic and priestly offices attached to the forgiveness of sins. He fulfilled the prophetic office not by pronouncing when God had already forgiven sins, like Samuel, Nathan, and Huldah, but, since he was God, by words in which he both *pointed* to the forgiveness of sins and *made it happen.*

Notice, in the assigned passage from Luke, the same pattern here as we saw in the Old Testament. A woman has sinned. She comes to God in sorrow for her sins and accepts the consequences of them. God forgives her. Notice also, however, where the story differs from the Old Testament. The prophets in the Old Testament all deferred to God concerning the forgiveness of sin. Nathan, Samuel, and Huldah could have said that the Lord had forgiven her sins, but they never could have turned to her like Jesus did and say with their own authority, "Your sins are forgiven."

Jesus fulfilled the priestly office not by performing a sacrifice that *represented* the repentance of God's people, but by performing one that actually *caused* it. St. Paul describes the parallel between Jesus' sacrifice on the Cross and the atonement liturgy in the Old Testament.

> But when Christ appeared as a high priest of the good things that have come, then through the greater and more perfect tent (not made with hands, that is, not of this creation) he entered once for all into the Holy Place, taking not the blood of goats and calves but his own blood, thus securing an eternal redemption. For if the sprinkling of defiled persons with the blood of goats and bulls and with the ashes of a heifer sanctifies for the purification of the flesh, how much more shall the blood of Christ, who through the eternal Spirit offered himself without blemish to God, purify your conscience from dead works to serve the living God. (Heb 9:11–14)

Through his sacrifice that sends the Holy Spirit upon the world, Jesus offers his people not only an outward liturgy, such as the people of Israel performed on the Day of Atonement, but an inward transformation.

As with the other sacraments, Jesus does not keep the power to forgive sins to himself. Just as he sends his disciples out to baptize, clothes them with the Holy Spirit to confirm, and commands them at the Last Supper to offer the Eucharist, so also does he give them the power to pronounce his words of forgiveness. The Scriptures refer to this several times. The first time is at the confession of Peter in the Gospel of Matthew. When Jesus gives Peter the keys to the kingdom of heaven, he tells Peter, "whatever you bind on earth shall be bound in heaven, and whatever you loose on earth shall be loosed in heaven" (Matt 16:19). Later in the Gospel when Jesus confers this same power upon the other future Apostles, he makes it clear that he is referring to the binding and loosing of sins:

> If your brother sins against you, go and tell him his fault, between you and him alone. If he listens to you, you have gained your brother. But if he does not listen, take one or two others along with you, that every word may be confirmed by the evidence of two or three witnesses. If he refuses to listen to them, tell it to the Church; and if he refuses to listen even to the Church, let him be to you as a Gentile and a tax collector. Truly, I say to you, whatever you bind on earth shall be bound in heaven, and whatever you loose on earth shall be loosed in heaven. Again I say to you, if two of you agree on earth about anything they ask, it will be done for them by my Father in heaven. For where two or three are gathered in my name, there am I in the midst of them. (Matt 18:15–20)

In Matthew's Gospel, Jesus' statements about binding and loosing have the character of a promise. In both cases, Jesus uses the future tense: whatever you bind on earth *shall* be bound in heaven; whatever you loose on earth *shall* be loosed in heaven. The fulfillment of that promise occurs after the Resurrection and is recorded in John's Gospel:

> On the evening of that day, the first day of the week, the doors being shut where the disciples were, for fear of the Jews, Jesus came and stood among them and said to them, "Peace be with you." When he had said this, he showed them his hands and his side. Then the disciples were glad when they saw the Lord. Jesus said to them again, "Peace be with you. As the Father has sent me, even so I send you." And when he had said this, he breathed on them, and said to them, "Receive the Holy Spirit. If you forgive the sins of any, they are forgiven; if you retain the sins of any, they are retained." (John 20:19–23)

After the Resurrection, when Jesus gives the Holy Spirit to the Apostles, he speaks in the present tense. Instead of saying, "If you forgive the sins of any, they *will be* forgiven," he says, "If you forgive the sins of any, they *are* forgiven." From that point forward, the Apostles, their successors, and those delegated by them received from Jesus the power to speak his words of forgiveness; and since Jesus is God, those words not only *point to* forgiveness, they *make it happen.*

The Apostles were faithful to the charge that they received from Jesus to forgive sins, even after Baptism. The Acts of the Apostles records that in Ephesus the Apostle Paul had the opportunity to administer this sacrament. The people in Ephesus had a history of engaging in magic arts and divination. After an extraordinary sign, in which the demons themselves acknowledged the power of Jesus and of Paul (Acts 19:15), the Scriptures tell us that there were many believers—people who had already been baptized—who had been practicing divination, which is a very grave sin (CCC 2116). Following the extraordinary sign from the demons, these people decided finally to repent from their sin. This was a great victory for God:

> Many also of those who were now believers came, confessing and divulging their practices. And a number of those who practiced magic arts brought their books together and burned them in the sight of all; and they counted the value of them and found it came to fifty thousand pieces of silver. So the word of the Lord grew and prevailed mightily. (Acts 19:18–20)

Notice how this follows the same pattern we have seen in the Old Testament, but with the Apostle now exercising the ministry for which Jesus commissioned him. There is a sin, God convicts the people of their sin, they confess their sin sincerely and accept the consequences, and God forgives their sin. So it was in the early Church, and so it is today.

History and Theology

|| ASSIGNED READING
|| CCC 1422–1498

Over the course of the centuries, the Church has developed its customary practice with regard to the Sacrament of Penance and Reconciliation (CCC 1447). In the Patristic period, the sacrament was offered with less frequency and only for more serious sins. A person looking to receive this sacrament would have to confess his or her sin(s) to a priest and would be enrolled in the "Order of Penitents" for some length of time, usually several years. During those years, the person would sit in a special section in the Church reserved for penitents and would be excluded from Communion. Only after the conclusion of the period of penance would a person finally be readmitted to Communion.

Given the length of time it took to complete penance and the desire of the faithful to receive the Eucharist again, two major developments took place in the life of the Church over the succeeding centuries. First, people sought ways of shortening their time of penance. One way in which they might seek a shortening of their time of penance was through the intercession of someone who was to be martyred. If that person were willing to offer up their martyrdom for the penance due the penitent's sin(s), the would-be martyr might write a document, called a *libellus*, which certified to the local bishop that they were intending to do so, and requested that the bishop lift the penitential period for the penitent. In response to the *libellus*, the bishop would sometimes grant a "remission" or "forgiveness" of the penance. In Latin, one word for pardon is *indulgentia*, and this became known as an *indulgence*.

Indulgences became and still are a regular part of the Church's ministry of forgiveness.

> An indulgence is a remission before God of the temporal punishment due to sins whose guilt has already been forgiven, which the faithful Christian who is duly disposed gains under certain prescribed conditions through the action of the Church

which, as the minister of redemption, dispenses and applies with authority the treasury of the satisfactions of Christ and the saints [Paul VI, Apostolic Constitution, *Indulgentiarum doctrina*, Norm 1]. (CCC 1471)

While the Sacrament of Penance and Reconciliation forgives the *eternal* consequences of our sins—separation from God—the purpose of an indulgence is to forgive part or all of the *temporal* consequences of our sins—those fitting consequences by which we are healed from the effects of our sin and taught not to sin again (CCC 1472). When Jesus conferred upon the Church the power to forgive sins, he did not specify that he was only conferring on the Church the power to forgive the eternal consequences of sins. Much to the contrary; he conferred upon the Church the power to forgive *all* the consequences of sin.

Indulgences are not a *substitute* for the Sacrament of Reconciliation; they are a *complement* to and a *completion* of it. In order to gain an indulgence, a person must be baptized, not excommunicated, and in a state of grace, which they obtain through the Sacrament of Penance and Reconciliation.[2] A person is then able to gain an indulgence for himself or for a soul in Purgatory by performing some action to which the Church has attached an indulgence. In addition to a number of special indulgences, the Church generally attaches an indulgence to prayer, fasting, almsgiving, and bearing public witness to the Catholic faith.[3]

The second major development to the Church's celebration of the Sacrament of Penance and Reconciliation was a move away from the celebration of public, long, and infrequent penance to private, short, and frequent penance. This occurred in the Latin Rite from about the seventh century onwards under the influence of Irish monks, although there are witnesses to it during the Patristic period in the East.[4] The celebration of the sacrament privately had a number of advantages: it

---

2   Catholic Church, *Enchiridion Indulgentiarum*, N. 17, §1.

3   Catholic Church, "Quattuor Concessiones Generaliores," in *Enchiridion Indulgentiarum*.

4   Theodore of Mopsuestia, "Baptismal Homily III," in Edward Yarnold, *The Awe-Inspiring Rites of Initiation: The Origins of RCIA* (Collegeville: Liturgical Press, 1994), 180–250.

enabled it to be celebrated more frequently, which meant that, practically speaking, it could be celebrated for venial sins as well as mortal ones. It also meant that, since each celebration of the sacrament did not cover as long a period in a person's life, it might not always require such lengthy penances. Finally, it meant that the faithful could more easily prepare for the celebration of the Eucharist, and it paved the way for the present custom of frequent—even daily—Communion.

QUESTIONS FOR REVIEW

1. What role did the prophets of ancient Israel play in helping people understand their sins?
2. What role did the priests of ancient Israel play in helping people atone for their sins?
3. How did Jesus fulfill the roles of both prophet and priest in regard to sin?
4. What power regarding sin did Jesus give to his Apostles?
5. What are indulgences and how do they help us?

QUESTIONS FOR DISCUSSION

1. Have you ever "hidden" from God when you have committed a sin? If so, what about God's love and mercy were you having a hard time seeing?
2. Have you ever thought about gaining an indulgence? How could you make indulgences a more regular part of your life with God?

Chapter 2

LIVING THE SACRAMENT

|| ASSIGNED READING
|| CIC, Canons 959–997

Celebration and Effects

In spite of developments concerning indulgences and private confession, the Sacrament of Penance and Reconciliation always followed the same basic pattern (CCC 1448). In the Middle Ages, theologians discerned that pattern by enumerating what they called the "Parts of Penance": contrition, confession, and satisfaction. In the most basic form of the Sacrament of Penance and Reconciliation, a person goes before a priest, expresses contrition for his or her sins, confesses all his or her mortal sins in name and number along with any venial sins that he or she may wish to confess, and makes a firm resolution to make satisfaction for those sins. The priest, after giving the person some spiritual counsel and advice, imposes upon that person a penance as the beginning of satisfaction for those sins and then grants the person the absolution of his or her sins.

"Contrition" is "'sorrow of the soul and detestation for the sin committed, together with the resolution not to sin again' [Council of Trent (1551): DS 1676]" (CCC 1451). There are two kinds of contrition: perfect contrition and imperfect contrition. Perfect contrition does not mean being as contrite as possible. In Latin, *perfecta* refers to something that is complete because it has all its parts. Perfect contrition is complete contrition. It is sorrow for our sins that is completed by the right motivation, the love of God, and the desire to confess our sins in the Sacrament of Penance and Reconciliation as soon as possible (CCC 1452). Imperfect contrition is also called "attrition." Attrition is imperfect because it is not completed by the love of God; it is motivated by the fear of God's punishments for sin instead (CCC 1453).

Attrition never obtains the remission of sins; it is completed and made into perfect contrition through the Sacrament of Penance and Reconciliation. On the other hand, since perfect contrition is motivated by the love of God, and since that love is caused in us by the Holy Spirit's presence, someone who has perfect contrition actually receives the forgiveness of their sins *before* approaching the sacrament.

Even if it is possible that a given individual, through perfect contrition, could obtain the forgiveness of mortal sins outside of the Sacrament of Penance and Reconciliation, there are three reasons why we should never presume that our post-baptismal sins are forgiven without the sacrament.

First, no one can love God without desiring at least implicitly the means by which God has chosen to forgive their sins; perfect contrition that obtains the forgiveness of mortal sins "includes the firm resolution to have recourse to sacramental confession as soon as possible [Cf. Council of Trent (1551): DS 1677]" (CCC 1452).

Second, only God knows our hearts. We can never be absolutely sure that our sorrow for sin is motivated purely by love and not in some way by fear; likewise we can never be absolutely sure that our resolution to go to the sacrament is firm enough. Much like a Baptism of Desire, we can be sure that if we have the proper kind of perfect contrition, then God will offer us the grace of forgiveness. But the only way we can be absolutely sure that God has offered us this grace is to go to the Sacrament of Penance and Reconciliation (CCC 1484).

Third, one who has received charity in his or her heart outside of the Sacrament of Penance and Reconciliation has not therefore received reconciliation with the Church. Since Jesus gave the power of binding and loosing to his Church (Matt 16:19; 18:18), only those who approach the Sacrament of Penance and Reconciliation are restored to complete Eucharistic fellowship in the Church. That is why the Church requires that

> a person who is conscious of grave sin is not to celebrate Mass or receive the body of the Lord without previous sacramental confession unless there is a grave reason and there is no opportunity to confess; in this case the person is to remember the obligation to make an act of perfect contrition which includes the resolution of confessing as soon as possible. (CIC, Canon 916)

If we want to be sure that God has offered us the forgiveness of our sins, and if we want to be permitted to receive the Eucharist when we are conscious of any grave sin, we should go to the Sacrament of Penance and Reconciliation.

"Confession" is the vocal disclosure of our sins to a priest in the Sacrament of Penance and Reconciliation.

> A member of the Christian faithful is obliged to confess in kind and number all grave sins committed after Baptism and not yet remitted directly through the keys of the Church nor acknowledged in individual confession, of which the person has knowledge after diligent examination of conscience. (CIC, Canon 988, §1)

The reason that we have to confess all of our mortal sins in kind and number is that we cannot have perfect contrition without it. Remember, perfect contrition only brings with it the forgiveness of our sins if it includes the resolution to confess our sins in the Sacrament of Penance and Reconciliation as soon as possible. We cannot receive the forgiveness of our sins, whether inside or outside the sacrament, without that kind of contrition. If we hold some sins back and do not disclose them, then we cannot receive forgiveness even for the ones we do disclose, because we lack the contrition necessary for forgiveness (see CCC 1456). Like the person who receives the Eucharist but is not in a state of grace, we commit the sin of sacrilege, and this adds to our souls another sin that separates us from the love of God and that also needs to be forgiven through the Sacrament of Penance and Reconciliation.

Nevertheless, we need not be troubled by disclosing even the most personal or embarrassing of sins, for "it is absolutely forbidden for a confessor to betray in any way a penitent in words or in any manner and for any reason" (CIC, Canon 983, §1; CCC 1467). It is similarly forbidden for a priest to make use of any knowledge he has gained through the sacrament to the detriment of a person who confesses to him (CIC, Canon 984, §1). A priest who directly violates this seal of the sacrament is automatically excommunicated and can only be re-admitted to Communion by the pope himself (CIC, Canon 1388, §1).

"Satisfaction" is making up for our sins wherever this needs to be done. Every sin harms our relationship with God, damages our relationship to our neighbors in the Church, and has a negative effect on ourselves. Some sins harm our neighbor(s) directly and concretely as well. This is easiest to understand if we consider an example, like stealing. If you knowingly and willingly steal a hundred dollars from your neighbor, the first thing you do is wound your relationship with God. Stealing violates the Seventh Commandment; as such it is grave matter for sin. If you do it knowingly and willingly, you lose the presence of the Holy Spirit in your soul and the grace that comes with it. By losing the presence of the Holy Spirit in your soul, you also lose the fullness of your relationship to the Church, which is bound together by that Spirit. What is more, you harm yourself. By giving in to an evil choice, you take the first step toward building a habit of bad choices; stealing here, cheating there, and then . . . who knows? Finally, you do direct, concrete harm to your neighbor—he's missing a hundred dollars.

In order to make satisfaction for your sin, you need to make it up to God, to the Church, to yourself, and to your neighbor. That's a lot of making up to do! If it were entirely up to us, no one could figure out and do everything it took to make up for our sins. It is only because Jesus has already offered satisfaction for our sins to the Father on the Cross, and because we are joined to that Cross by the Holy Spirit through Baptism— and again through the Sacrament of Penance and Reconciliation—that, empowered by Jesus working in us through his Holy Spirit, we can make up for our sins *with* Jesus.

The first thing we need to do is make it up to God. We do this by willingly accepting, like Adam, Eve, and Saul, all the consequences that God gives us for our sins and by performing other good actions that we offer God as penance for our sins (CCC 1459). The second thing we need to do is make it up to the Church. We do this by willingly accepting and performing the penance that the priest imposes upon us in the Sacrament of Penance and Reconciliation (CCC 1460; CIC, Canon 981). While the penance imposed upon us is all that is required to make up for our sins to the Church, it can be, but is not necessarily, all that is required to make up for our sins to God; the goal of the penance imposed by the priest is to get us started in building a habit of penance and continual conversion of life, not to constitute all the penance that we ever need to do in our lives (see CCC 1431). The third thing we need to do is make it up to ourselves. We do this by willingly accepting God's consequences and the Church's penance, as well as by trying to find ways of building good habits to counteract our bad ones; if we've stolen something, we can make it up to ourselves by building a habit of just dealings with others. The fourth thing we need to do is make it up to our neighbor. He still needs his hundred dollars back. We need to make restitution to our neighbor by giving him back what we took from him and by apologizing for the harm done by it (CCC 2412).

As we saw above, the forgiveness of sins was entrusted by Jesus to his Apostles in the Gospels and was exercised by them in the early Church. Consequently, bishops, as successors of the Apostles, are the primary authority by whom the Sacrament of Penance and Reconciliation is celebrated. However, since the forgiveness of sins is a priestly ministry, any priest has the power to celebrate the Sacrament of Penance and Reconciliation, provided that he has received appropriate permission to do so (CCC 1462; CIC, Canons 965–975). In danger of death, the Church gives every priest that permission (CIC, Canon 976).

When a person goes to the Sacrament of Penance and Reconciliation, shows contrition, makes confession, and resolves to make satisfaction for his or her sins, the minister of the sacrament grants him or her "absolution" by speaking the Words of Absolution, which are the words of Jesus, over the penitent: "I absolve you." In the Latin Rite, those words are said in the context of the following prayer:

> God, the Father of mercies,
> through the death and the resurrection of his Son
> has reconciled the world to himself
> and sent the Holy Spirit among us
> for the forgiveness of sins;
> through the ministry of the Church
> may God give you pardon and peace,
> and I absolve you from your sins
> in the name of the Father, and of the Son, and of the Holy
>   Spirit.[1]

When we receive absolution, the priest speaks the words of Jesus to us and, just as surely as the sins of the sinful woman were forgiven in the Gospel, ours are too. Absolution brings with it the forgiveness of all the eternal punishment due our mortal sins and part of the forgiveness of the temporal punishment due our sins. By thus paving the way for the Holy Spirit to come back into our hearts with his grace, it reconciles us with God and with our neighbors in the Church, puts our hearts and our consciences at ease, and it strengthens us to go forth and contend against temptation once more (CCC 1496). For this reason, "The fathers of the Church present this sacrament as 'the second plank [of salvation] after the shipwreck which is the loss of grace' [Tertullian, *De Paenit.* 4, 2: PL 1, 1343; cf. Council of Trent (1547): DS 1542]" (CCC 1446).

In addition to celebrations of the Sacrament of Penance and Reconciliation, which take place privately and individually, there are two other ways in which the Church can grant us sacramental absolution. The first is in the context of a communal penance service. Such a service is not a form of group confession so much as a communal gathering in which the members of the community prepare together to make private and indi-

---

[1]   *Ordo Poenitentiae* 46, quoted in CCC 1449.

vidual confession, and then give thanks together for the forgiveness they received individually (CCC 1482).

It differs from General Confession and General Absolution, in which, owing to grave necessity, a priest grants absolution to a group of people all at once (CCC 1483). General Confession and General Absolution do grant the sacramental forgiveness of sins to those who undergo them. However, since the perfect contrition that brings with it the forgiveness of sins includes a resolution to make confession of one's sins in kind and number, and since the Church cannot change God's requirement that a person have perfect contrition in order to receive the forgiveness of sins, a person who receives General Absolution cannot have his or her sins forgiven unless he or she "at the same time intends to confess within a suitable period of time each grave sin which at the present time cannot be so confessed" (CIC, Canon 962, §1; see CCC 1483).

Appropriating and Living This Sacrament

As mentioned above, the Sacrament of Penance and Reconciliation is not the end of healing from sin; it is the beginning. When we come forth from confessing our sins, we begin a new life of grace, but we may still have quite a bit of the old life yet to make up for. The first step in appropriating and living the Sacrament of Penance and Reconciliation is therefore to make sure that we diligently and lovingly attend to all that is required of us to make up for our sins to God, to his Church, to ourselves, and to our neighbors. We should pray, fast, and give alms to make up to God for our sins; we may even seek to gain an indulgence by these actions to help us make up for our sins to God more quickly and completely. We should promptly and completely fulfill the penance imposed upon us by the priest who celebrated the sacrament with us to make up for our sins to the Church. We should find ways of doing good to counteract the negative effects of our sins and to make up for our sins to ourselves. Finally, we should be sure to make restitution to our neighbors for any moral or physical harm we may have done them.

Provided that we do our best to make up for our old life, we should welcome and embrace with joy the new life that the Sacrament of Penance and Reconciliation gives us so that we may build a habit of living out this new life with joy and thanksgiving. We can start this new life right away by making an Act of Thanksgiving after we receive the sacrament, thanking God for welcoming us once again into his friendship and coming to make his home in our hearts. We can continue this new life by asking for and accepting from God ever more deeply the grace of conversion. Conversion is when we turn away from sin. In one sense, our conversion happens at our Baptism as well as every time we go to the Sacrament of Penance and Reconciliation (CCC 1427). But in another sense, conversion is the whole task of a Christian life, because however much we have turned away from sin, we can always turn away from it a bit more; however much we have turned toward God, we can always turn toward him a bit more (CCC 1428).

Finally, there is no better way to appropriate and live the Sacrament of Penance and Reconciliation than by approaching the other sacrament for which it prepares us, the Sacrament of the Eucharist (CCC 1436). Through absolution, we are brought once more into friendship and fellowship with Jesus and we are prepared to renew the covenant that we have with him in his Body and Blood. When we faithfully approach the Sacrament of the Eucharist after having been forgiven in the Sacrament of Penance and Reconciliation, Jesus rejoices to be united with us once more, even as the Father and all the angels and saints rejoice at our return to him from whom we had gone astray (Luke 15:7).

SELECTED READING
Council of Trent, Decree on the Most Holy Sacraments of Penance and Extreme Unction, "Doctrine on the Sacrament of Penance," chaps. 1–3

CHAPTER I. On the necessity, and on the institution of the Sacrament of Penance
If such, in all the regenerate, were their gratitude towards God, as that they constantly preserved the justice received in baptism by

His bounty and grace; there would not have been need for another sacrament, besides that of baptism itself, to be instituted for the remission of sins. But because God, rich in mercy, knows our frame, He hath bestowed a remedy of life even on those who may, after baptism, have delivered themselves up to the servitude of sin and the power of the devil—the sacrament to wit of Penance, by which the benefit of the death of Christ is applied to those who have fallen after baptism.

Penitence was in deed at all times necessary, in order to attain to grace and justice, for all men who had defiled themselves by any mortal sin, even for those who begged to be washed by the sacrament of Baptism; that so, their perverseness renounced and amended, they might, with a hatred of sin and a godly sorrow of mind, detest so great an offence of God. Wherefore the prophet says, "Be converted and do penance for all your iniquities, and iniquity shall not be your ruin." The Lord also said; "Except you do penance, you shall also likewise perish"; and Peter, the prince of the apostles, recommending penitence to sinners who were about to be initiated by baptism, said; "Do penance, and be baptized every one you."

Nevertheless, neither before the coming of Christ was penitence a sacrament, nor is it such, since His coming, to any previously to baptism. But the Lord then principally instituted the sacrament of penance, when, being raised from the dead, He breathed upon His disciples, saying "Receive ye the Holy Ghost, whose sins you shall forgive, they are forgiven them, and whose sins you shall retain, they are retained." By which action so signal, and words so clear, the consent of all the Fathers has ever understood, that the power of forgiving and retaining sins was communicated to the apostles and their lawful successors, for the reconciling of the faithful who have fallen after baptism. And the Catholic Church with great reason repudiated and condemned as heretics, the Novatians, who of old obstinately denied that power of forgiving. Wherefore, this holy Synod, approving of and receiving as most true this meaning of those words of our Lord, condemns the fanciful interpretations of those who, in opposition to the institution of this sacrament, falsely wrest those words to the power of preaching the word of God, and of announcing the Gospel of Christ.

CHAPTER II. On the difference between the Sacrament of Penance and that of Baptism

For the rest, this sacrament is clearly seen to be different from baptism in many respects: for besides that it is very widely different indeed in matter and form, which constitute the essence of a sacrament, it is beyond doubt certain that the minister of baptism need not be a judge, seeing that the Church exercises judgment on no one who has not entered therein through the gate of baptism. For, what have I, saith the apostle, to do to judge them that are without? It is otherwise with those who are of the household of the faith, whom Christ our Lord has once, by the laver of baptism, made the members of His own body; for such, if they should afterwards have defiled themselves by any crime, He would no longer have them cleansed by a repetition of baptism—that being nowise lawful in the Catholic Church—but be placed as criminals before this tribunal; that, by the sentence of the priests, they might be freed, not once, but as often as, being penitent, they should, from their sins committed, flee thereunto. Furthermore, one is the fruit of baptism, and another that of penance. For, by baptism putting on Christ, we are made therein entirely a new creature, obtaining a full and entire remission of all sins: unto which newness and entireness, however, we are no ways able to arrive by the sacrament of Penance, without many tears and great labours on our parts, the divine justice demanding this; so that penance has justly been called by holy Fathers a laborious kind of baptism. And this sacrament of Penance is, for those who have fallen after baptism, necessary unto salvation; as baptism itself is for those who have not as yet been regenerated.

CHAPTER III. On the parts, and on the fruit of this Sacrament

The holy synod doth furthermore teach, that the form of the sacrament of penance, wherein its force principally consists, is placed in those words of the minister, I absolve thee, etc., to which words indeed certain prayers are, according to the custom of holy Church, laudably joined, which nevertheless by no means regard the essence of that form, neither are they necessary for the administration of the sacrament itself. But the acts of the penitent himself, to wit, contrition, confession and satisfaction, are as it were the matter of this sacrament. Which acts, inasmuch as they are, by God's institution, required in the penitent for the integrity of the sacrament, and for the full and perfect remission of sins, are for this reason called the parts of penance. But the thing signified indeed and the effect of this sacrament, as far as regards its force and efficacy, is reconciliation with God, which sometimes, in persons who are pious and who receive this sacrament with devotion, is wont to be followed by peace and serenity of conscience, with exceeding consolation of spirit. The holy Synod, whilst delivering these things touching the parts and the effect of this sacrament, condemns at the same time the opinions of those who contend, that, the terrors which agitate the conscience, and faith, are the parts of penance.

QUESTIONS FOR REVIEW

1. Name and define each of the three "parts" of Confession.
2. What is the difference between perfect and imperfect contrition?
3. Who is the minister of the Sacrament of Confession?
4. Why do we need to make satisfaction for our sins?
5. What is the difference between General Confession and General Absolution? Under what circumstances can General Absolution be offered?

QUESTIONS FOR DISCUSSION

1. Do you struggle with going to Confession regularly? Why or why not?
2. Even though going to Confession can feel hard or embarrassing at first, many people feel deep relief and joy afterward. Where does that joy come from? How can you share it with others in your life?

Part VI

ANOINTING OF THE SICK

The Sacrament of the Anointing of the Sick is the fifth of the seven sacraments and the second Sacrament of Healing. In its most basic form, a priest anoints a person with oil blessed by a bishop and prays over the sick person, "Through this holy anointing may the Lord in his love and mercy help you with the grace of the Holy Spirit. May the Lord who frees you from sin save you and raise you up [Cf. CIC, Can. 847 § 1]" (CCC 1513). The sick person is strengthened by the gift of the Holy Spirit and cleansed of any remnants of sin that may still remain after the Sacrament of Penance and Reconciliation.

Chapter 1

UNDERSTANDING THE SACRAMENT

Old Testament

|| ASSIGNED READING
|| Leviticus 14

When we were discussing the Sacrament of Penance and Reconciliation, we noted previously that the "death" that Adam and Eve received when they ate of the fruit of the Tree of the Knowledge of Good and Evil was spiritual death: the separation of the soul from God. But that was not the only death to which they were now subject. Even if Adam and Eve did not undergo physical death in that moment, they became subject to it when they could no longer eat of the fruit of the Tree of Life. Without that fruit to sustain them, they could suffer illness, old age, and, ultimately, bodily death (CCC 1500–1501).

From the time that God began to restore spiritual life in his people by making covenants with them, God also took an interest in restoring their physical life by healing them from their sicknesses (CCC 1502). The first sickness in the Bible is the infertility suffered by Abram's wife, Sarai (Gen 11:30). Barrenness, as the Scriptures call it, was a particularly painful illness. It was painful on a natural level to be deprived of children.

It was also painful on a spiritual level because it was the direct consequence of losing the original blessing that God gave to humanity: "And
God blessed them, and God said to them, 'Be fruitful and multiply, and
fill the earth and subdue it'" (Gen 1:28). Not that Sarai committed some
personal sin by which she was stricken with barrenness; rather, as a result
of being born in a state without that original blessing, she, like everyone
else, was subject to the possibility of it.

As part of healing Abram's and Sarai's spiritual relationship with God,
God decided that he would heal Sarai's body (Gen 18:10). The healing
of her body had a spiritual purpose. By trusting the Lord to be faithful to
his promise of children, Abram and Sarai would receive back some of the
blessing that Adam and Eve had lost. Neither Abram nor Sarai trusted
God perfectly. Abram questioned God (Gen 15:8) and then had a child
with Sarai's handmaid; Sarai figured that this must have been what God
actually meant (Gen 16:2). Sarai also laughed at an angel of God when
she overheard it insisting to Abram that she herself would bear a child
(Gen 18:12–15).

God did heal Sarai, whom he renamed Sarah, and she became the
mother of Isaac (Gen 21:1–2). Isaac was himself one of the direct ances-
tors of Jesus. Along the way, there were many other miraculous births that
prefigured the restoration of the blessing that humanity had lost with
Adam and Eve's first sin: that of Joseph from Rachel (Gen 30:22–23),
Samson from the wife of Zorah (Judg 13:2–25), Samuel from Hannah (1
Sam 1), and John the Baptist from Elizabeth (Luke 1:5–25).

Under the Mosaic Law, healing had a similarly spiritual dimension.
We see this most clearly in the case of leprosy. Leprosy (or Hansen's
Disease, as it is now known) is a bacterial infection that corrodes the skin
and outer limbs of a person until the person dies. Until the discovery
of the bacteria that causes it in 1873 and the development of suitable
antibiotics, there was no cure. Unless a person was healed by God naturally or miraculously, the person would eventually die from it and could
infect others with the disease. For this reason, in ancient times such a
person was usually excluded from the corporate assemblies of the people
of Israel, including their gatherings for worship. They were understood
to be ritually "unclean" (Lev 13:3).

It did sometimes happen, however, that a person would recover from leprosy or a related disease. Given the gravity of the disease and the rarity of the event, this was experienced as a palpable blessing from God. It meant that the person was not only restored to physical health, like the women who received miraculous children, but that he or she was restored to the blessings of health that belonged to humanity in paradise. What is more, he or she could be pronounced ritually "clean" and restored to the communal worship of God with his or her fellow Israelites.

There was a special liturgy prescribed in the Mosaic Law for people that were cured of leprosy in order to examine them and to pronounce them ritually clean. It took place in two stages. In the first stage, a person was pronounced clean and readmitted to the camp, but was not allowed into his tent (Lev 14:1–9). In the second stage, the person underwent a complete ritual cleansing, that included both blood and oil, and afterward was fully allowed back to his home (Lev 14:10–20).

It is important for us to note, however, that these ritual washings did not cause the healing of that sickness, nor did they cause the forgiveness of the remnants of sin associated with it. As signs of the Old Testament, they could only point to healing and forgiveness but they could not cause it. Consequently, we cannot say that the priests of the Old Testament healed lepers. Rather, they certified when God had healed lepers, whether naturally or miraculously, and they restored those whom God had healed first to the community and then to their homes.

New Testament

ASSIGNED READING
Matthew 8:1–4
James 5:14–15

In the New Testament, the Holy Spirit shows us the continuity of God's healing work from Isaac, Joseph, Samson, Samuel, and John to Jesus by bringing forth the Son of God miraculously from the womb of the Blessed Virgin Mary. This is itself a kind of healing. But it is not a healing in the UNDERSTANDING THE SACRAMENT

same way that Sarah, Rachel, the wife of Zorah, Hannah, and Elizabeth were healed of infertility. Mary was immaculately conceived; she was healed *in the most perfect way* by being preserved from all stain of original sin from the first moment of her conception (CCC 491). In her, *human nature itself* was healed, and from her came forth the healer of us all.

Just as Jesus shows himself to be God by forgiving sins, so also does Jesus show himself to be God by healing people from sickness and from the ultimate effect of sickness, physical death (CCC 1503). Nowhere is this more apparent than in his healing of lepers.

The first major healing that Jesus performs happens after the Sermon on the Mount (Matt 5–7). In that sermon, Jesus shows himself to be the fulfillment of everything that the Mosaic Law looked forward to (Matt 5:17). That includes the fulfillment of the cleansing of lepers; and so it is no accident that as soon as Jesus comes down from the mountain, the first thing he does is heal a leper (Matt 8:1–4).

As with his other offices, Jesus does not keep the power of healing from sin and sickness to himself; he shares it with his disciples (CCC 1504, 1509). Mark tells us that when Jesus sent out his disciples into the world they performed signs similar to the ones Jesus did; they "anointed with oil many that were sick and healed them" (Mark 6:13). Notice that Mark speaks of the disciples more like Jesus and less like Mosaic priests. In the Old Testament, only God heals; in the New Testament, Jesus heals because he is God, and Mark tells us that when Jesus sent out his disciples, *they healed.*

After the Resurrection, when Jesus breathed the Holy Spirit upon the Apostles to confirm them in their sacramental ministry, James tells us that Jesus instituted a special sacrament so that the Church could continue healing people from the effects of sickness and death, and preparing them to go home—home to heaven, that is.

> Is any among you sick? Let him call for the elders [presbyters] of the Church, and let them pray over him, anointing him with oil in the name of the Lord; and the prayer of faith will save the sick man, and the Lord will raise him up; and if he has committed sins, he will be forgiven. (Jas 5:14–15)

134

Let's read this text closely: First, if someone is sick, we are told that we should call for the presbyters of the Church. "Presbyter" is the word that the Scriptures use for someone of priestly dignity (CIC, Canon 1003). In the Old Testament, the priests pointed out healing. In the New Testament, the priests caused healing through a sacrament.

Then we are told that the priests should pray over the sick man. That makes this sacrament a little different than any other sacrament. In other sacraments, the minister of the sacrament speaks Jesus' words, and Jesus' words are a direct statement: "I *baptize* you," or, "This *is* my body." In this sacrament, the minister speaks Jesus' words and Jesus' words are a prayer:

> Through this holy anointing *may* the Lord in his love and mercy help you with the grace of the Holy Spirit. *May* the Lord who frees you from sin save you and raise you up. (CCC 1513, emphasis added)

Then we are told that the priests should anoint him with oil, just like the priests did in the Mosaic Law.

When a priest prays the prayer of Jesus and anoints the sick person with oil, we are told that, unlike many other prayers we might pray, this prayer "will save the sick man." The text expresses confidence that God will hear the priest's prayer because the priest is praying not just any prayer, but the words of God. God's words not only point to things, they make things happen, whether expressed directly or as a supplication.

Lastly, we are told that saving the sick man has two components: first, "the Lord will raise him up." Notice the text does not say, "he will get better." That's because God does not promise that people who receive the Sacrament of the Anointing of the Sick will get better from their sickness. "Raise him up" is a biblical term that usually refers to the resurrection from the dead on the last day. That's always the way that Jesus uses the phrase (John 6:40, 44, 54). When James promises that those who receive the sacrament will be raised up, what he means is that the sacrament will prepare them for the final resurrection because it will give them the grace to go home—home to heaven to be with Jesus.

The means by which the sacrament will "raise him up" are stated in the next phrase: "If he has committed sins, he will be forgiven." The sacrament raises up the sick person by cleansing him or her of sin and its remains. In this way, it does what the liturgy of the cleansing of lepers never could:

> The Jewish priests had authority to release the body from leprosy, or, rather, not to release it but only to examine those who were already released, and you know how much the office of priest was contended for at that time. But our priests have received authority to deal, not with bodily leprosy, but spiritual uncleanness—not to pronounce it removed after examination, but actually and absolutely to take it away.

> Our natural parents generate us unto this life only, but the others [our priests] unto that which is to come. And the former would not be able to avert death from their offspring, or to repel the assaults of disease; but these others have often saved a sick soul, or one which was on the point of perishing, procuring for some a milder chastisement, and preventing others from falling altogether, not only by instruction and admonition, but also by the assistance wrought through prayers. For not only at the time of regeneration, but afterwards also, they have authority to forgive sins. "Is any sick among you?" it is said, "let him call for the elders of the Church and let them pray over him, anointing him with oil in the name of the Lord. And the prayer of faith shall save the sick, and the Lord will raise him up: and if he have committed sins they shall be forgiven him" (Jas 5:14–15). Again: our natural parents, should their children come into conflict with any men of high rank and great power in the world, are unable to profit them: but priests have reconciled, not rulers and kings, but God Himself when His wrath has often been provoked against them.[1]

---

[1]   St. John Chrysostom, *On the Priesthood* 3.6 (NPNF 1.9:47–48).

There is one exception to the general rule about being raised up. We are told that when Peter took a lame man by the hand and healed him, he "raised up" the lame man. For that reason, we can say that being "raised up" can, but does not have to, mean being healed bodily. Nevertheless, it always means being healed spiritually and being prepared to be raised up with the saints in glory on the last day (CCC 1509).

History and Theology

|| ASSIGNED READING
|| CCC 1499–1535

"From ancient times in the liturgical traditions of both East and West, we have testimonies to the practice of anointing of the sick with blessed oil," says the Catechism (1512). There have, however, been variations as to when this sacrament has been administered to the sick, as well as in what relation to the other sacraments it has been administered. All of these variations have had one goal: to prepare people best to go home to heaven. For this reason, the Church's understanding of the sacrament and its relationship to the Scriptures has remained constant, even if the practice of administering the sacrament has changed from time to time.

As we have seen, the Sacrament of Anointing of the Sick prepares people to go home in two ways: it cleanses them from sin and its remains, and it thereby prepares their bodies for the final resurrection. It may also, but need not, heal the bodily infirmity from which they are presently suffering. Sometimes the Church has emphasized cleansing of sin in the administration of the sacrament; other times it has emphasized preparation for the bodily resurrection and healing from bodily infirmities.

By the time of the Middle Ages, Chrysostom's understanding of the sacrament as forgiving sins became the more common emphasis. In this context, the sacrament was seen as a completion and a complement of the Sacrament of Penance and Reconciliation. Just as the Sacrament of Penance and Reconciliation cleanses us of mortal sin, so also does this sacrament cleanse us of what remains after the forgiveness of our mortal sins. This emphasis on the sacrament's ability to forgive sin, while not totally separated from an understanding of the sacrament's ability to heal, did lead to a particular pastoral practice as concerns the last sacraments a person is given before departing this life. Since, in order to go home to heaven rather than be detained in purgatory, a person must be cleansed of all the remnants of sin, the administration of the sacrament was reserved to the last moments of a dying person's life. For that reason, it was typically referred to as the Sacrament of Extreme Unction. "Unction" means "anointing." The word "extreme" is from the Latin *in extremis*, meaning "at the moment of death."

> Each sacrament was instituted for one effect in particular, although it may also be able to exhibit other effects which follow from that one. And since a sacrament "causes what it represents," its principal effect should be taken from the very sign which belongs to the sacrament. Now, this sacrament [Extreme Unction] is applied in the manner of a kind of medicine, just as Baptism is applied in the manner of a bath; but the purpose of medicine is to take away sickness; therefore this sacrament was instituted principally to heal the sickness of sin, so that, just as Baptism is a kind of spiritual rebirth, and Penance is a kind of spiritual resuscitation, so also Extreme Unction is a kind of spiritual healing or medicine. [2]

As a result of emphasizing the sacrament's ability to forgive sin, the Church's pastoral practice for dying persons was as follows: first, the person was offered the Sacrament of Penance and Reconciliation. Provided that he was able to confess his sins, he was then offered Holy Communion as Viaticum so as to be united with Our Lord now that he was in a state of grace. Finally, he was given the Sacrament of Anointing of the Sick as a final preparation to enter our heavenly homeland.

While there is nothing wrong *per se* with waiting until the moment of death to give someone the Sacrament of Anointing of the Sick, there are

---

[2]   Aquinas, ST, Supplement, q. 30, a. 1, resp. (Leonine 12:57).

some difficulties that arise from this pastoral practice. The greatest difficulty is that many people on their deathbeds are not able to participate consciously in the reception of this sacrament. This can mean that they don't get to make as much use of the graces offered to them in the sacrament as they could have, had it been offered to them when they were conscious. A second difficulty is that, while miracles can and do occur, this leaves less opportunity in the ordinary course of things for the sacrament to achieve its healing effect in a more immediate sense without a dramatic miracle happening.

QUESTIONS FOR REVIEW

1. In the Old Testament, what did physical healing signify?
2. What two material substances were used in the Israelites' ritual cleansing ceremonies for lepers?
3. What does Jesus show us through the miraculous healings he performed?
4. Where in Sacred Scripture is the Sacrament of the Anointing of the Sick mentioned? How are we told it was celebrated by the Apostles?
5. What is the danger of waiting until the moment of death for the Sacrament of the Anointing of the Sick?

QUESTIONS FOR DISCUSSION

1. Have you ever been seriously injured or sick? If so, how was your illness or injury frustrating? How did God help you? If not, have you ever cared for someone else who was? What was that experience like?
2. Have you ever been in a situation when you needed to receive the Sacrament of Anointing of the Sick? If so, what was it like? If not, how can you prepare yourself now so that if such a situation ever arises, you're ready to accept all the graces that God wants to give you through it?

Chapter 2

LIVING THE SACRAMENT

|| ASSIGNED READING
|| CIC, Canons 998–1007

Celebration

After the Second Vatican Council, the Church changed its practice, but not its teaching, in the administration of the Sacrament of Anointing of the Sick. In order to foster more active participation in the people who receive the sacrament, as well as to emphasize the sacrament's ability to heal the body, the Church began administering the sacrament to people before they were at the moment of death—as soon as they started to become seriously sick. The official Latin word that the Church uses for "seriously" is *periculose*, which literally means "very dangerously" (CCC 1513; CIC, Canon 1004, §1). A person can be in this situation multiple times: "This sacrament can be repeated if the sick person, having recovered, again becomes gravely ill or if the condition becomes more grave during the same illness" (CIC, Canon 1004, §2).

The sacrament has not lost its connection with physical death, which is the consequence of sickness; rather, it now has a more holistic connection with both sickness and death and so can more easily be seen as applicable to both. It also more commonly affords the sick person the opportunity to participate consciously in the reception of the sacrament, and so it has been possible to add to this sacrament a celebration of the Liturgy of the Word (CCC 1518) and sometimes to celebrate it in community (CCC 1517; CIC, Canon 1002). "In a case of necessity, however, a single anointing on the forehead or even on some other part of the body is sufficient, while the entire formula is said" (CIC, Canon 1000, §1).

As a consequence of the Church's change of emphasis, the Church has also changed her pastoral practice for dying persons. Where previously the Church prepared people to go home by giving them the Sacrament of Anointing of the Sick as their last sacrament, now she prepares people to go home by giving them the Eucharist as Viaticum as their last sacrament after Anointing of the Sick (CCC 1517).

There is a very concrete benefit to this. The more charity we have in our hearts when we die, the greater will be our share in heavenly glory with Christ; the greatest increase of charity available to us in this life is through a worthy reception of Holy Communion. Therefore, the better our participation in our final Communion, the better will be our share in heavenly glory in the life to come; but the more perfectly cleansed from sin we are before our final Communion, the better will be our participation in it. There is no better preparation for our going home than for us first to be cleansed of the remnants of sin through the Sacrament of Anointing and then to be united with Jesus in Holy Communion. Moreover, this conforms better to the pattern of the Old Testament, in which lepers were cleansed first by a guilt offering, which prefigured the Sacrament of Penance and Reconciliation, then by anointing with blood and oil, which prefigured the Sacrament of Anointing of the Sick, and finally were prepared to go home by a sin offering, a burnt offering, and a cereal offering, which prefigured the Eucharist.

Effects of the Sacrament

In discussing the history of the Sacrament of Anointing of the Sick in Scripture and Tradition, we have already mentioned its effects. However, it will be useful to summarize them again here.

First, the sacrament unites us with the Blood of Christ (CCC 1521). The Blood of Christ replaces and fulfills the blood of the lamb that was sacrificed for the cleansing of lepers in the Old Testament.

Christ's Blood fills us with the Holy Spirit (CCC 1520). The Holy Spirit heals us from the remnants of sin and, where necessary, forgives any sins that may remain in us. This strengthens us to face the spiritual trials that sickness and death entail, prepares us for the final resurrection, and may—when beneficial to the soul—lead to the bodily healing of the present infirmity.

By cleansing our soul from sin, the Sacrament of Anointing of the Sick prepares us to go home to heaven:

> The Anointing of the Sick completes our conformity to the death and Resurrection of Christ, just as Baptism began it. It completes the holy anointings that mark the whole Christian life: that of Baptism which sealed the new life in us, and that of Confirmation which strengthened us for the combat of this life. This last anointing fortifies the end of our earthly life like a solid rampart for the final struggles before entering the Father's house [Council of Trent (1551): DS 1694]. (CCC 1523)

Lastly, when given to those who are dying, the Sacrament of Anointing of the Sick readies us to go home by preparing us for union with Jesus on earth through the worthy reception of the Eucharist as Viaticum. This in turn prepares us in a more immediate sense to meet Jesus in heaven.

Appropriating and Living This Sacrament

Owing to the connections between sickness and death, and to the fact that this sacrament is often administered to people who are dying, there is not always as much of an opportunity to live out this sacrament on earth after having received it as there is with the other six sacraments. In a real sense, we most properly live out this sacrament when, strengthened by its effects, we dwell with Christ forever in heaven, awaiting the resurrection of our bodies, when "What is sown is perishable, what is raised is imperishable" (1 Cor 15:42). However, there are ways in which we can live out this sacrament prior to its reception, as well as ways in which we can live it out after having received it in the time that the Lord grants us.

First and foremost, we can live out the reality of the Sacrament of Anointing of the Sick by uniting ourselves with the goal of the sacrament, using each day as a preparation to *go home* to heaven by avoiding sin and growing in charity. That is a daily decision and a daily battle; it is the struggle into which we are initiated by Baptism and for which we are empowered by Confirmation. But we are not without assistance in that struggle. Through the regular reception of the Sacrament of Penance and Reconciliation we are cleansed of sin; through the regular reception of the Eucharist we grow in charity. By participating actively and frequently in these two sacraments we anticipate the reality for which the Sacrament of the Anointing of the Sick will ultimately prepare us.

Second, we can unite ourselves with the *means* of the sacrament, seeking each day to join our sufferings to the Blood of Jesus poured out for us on the Cross. We do this first and foremost by "picking up our cross and following him" amidst the struggles that the illnesses and weaknesses of this life cause us (CCC 1506) and turning to Jesus whenever we feel sick or weak. Our trust in Jesus in these smaller sufferings prepares us to trust in Jesus in times of greater suffering, even in that last suffering wherein we prepare to depart from this life.

Third, we can unite ourselves with the possible *effect* of the sacrament: the healing of our bodies from present illness, if God wills. We do this by joyfully accepting the will of God for us each day, whether in health or sickness. This prepares us ultimately to accept from God in the celebration of the Sacrament of Anointing of the Sick whatever state of health God may will for us. And if he wills not to grant us healing from our present illness, to accept death at whatever time and in whatever way he may will for us, so that we may depart this life in complete union with the will of Jesus.

Fourth, we can unite ourselves with those who are receiving this sacrament, especially those who are dying. Like those who have yet to be born, the aged, infirm, and dying are among the most vulnerable members of society, and they face the increasing threat and pressure of euthanasia (CCC 2276–2279). By praying for them, we call down God's strength, help, and comfort upon them, and we take part in turning the hearts of those who wrongfully threaten to end their lives prematurely.

If we have received or do receive the Sacrament of Anointing of the Sick, all three of these practices will benefit us all the more. By avoiding sin and growing in charity—particularly through the worthy reception of the Eucharist—we are prepared for the very moment of death, at which "each man receives his eternal retribution in his immortal soul" (CCC 1022). By uniting ourselves with the Blood of Jesus, we cooperate with the grace offered to us in the sacrament to make our sufferings his sufferings and so to be strengthened and comforted by him in our illness illness. We also do this "to complete what is lacking in Christ's afflictions for the sake of his body, that is, the Church" (Col 1:24), making ourselves an instrument of Christ's grace by offering ourselves as a living sacrifice for those in need. Finally, by accepting the will of God for us, we open ourselves to profit from whatever gifts of grace God may will to give us in the moment of our sickness, be it the gift of bodily health in an immediate sense or a more direct preparation for the final resurrection in the life hereafter.

SELECTED READING
Pope Benedict XVI, Message on the Occasion of the
Twentieth World Day of the Sick (November 20, 2012),
introduction and nos. 1, 3

On the occasion of the World Day of the Sick, which we will celebrate on 11 February 2012, the Memorial of Our Lady of Lourdes, I wish to renew my spiritual closeness to all sick people who are in places of care or are looked after in their families, expressing to each one of them the solicitude and the affection of the whole Church. In the generous and loving welcoming of every human life, above all of weak and sick life, a Christian expresses an important aspect of his or her Gospel witness, following the example of Christ, who bent down before the material and spiritual sufferings of man in order to heal them.

This year, which involves the immediate preparations for the Solemn World Day of the Sick that will be celebrated in Germany on 11 February 2013 and will focus on the emblematic Gospel figure of the Good Samaritan (cf. *Lk* 10:29–37), I would like to place emphasis upon the "sacraments of healing," that is to say upon the sacrament of Penance and Reconciliation and that of the Anointing of the Sick, which have their natural completion in Eucharistic Communion.

The encounter of Jesus with the ten lepers, narrated by the Gospel of Saint Luke (cf. *Lk* 17:11–19), and in particular the words that the Lord addresses to one of them, "Stand up and go; your faith has saved you" (v. 19), help us to become aware of the importance of faith for those who, burdened by suffering and illness, draw near to the Lord. In their encounter with him they can truly experience that *he who believes is never alone*! God, indeed, in his Son, does not abandon us to our anguish and sufferings, but is close to us, helps us to bear them, and wishes to heal us in the depths of our hearts (cf. *Mk* 2:1–12).

The faith of the lone leper who, on seeing that he was healed, full of amazement and joy, and unlike the others, immediately went back to Jesus to express his gratitude, enables us to perceive that reacquired health is a sign of something more precious than mere physical healing, it is a sign of the salvation that God gives us through Christ; it finds expression in the words of Jesus: *your faith has saved you*. He who in suffering and illness prays to the Lord is certain that God's love will never abandon him, and also that the love of the Church, the extension in time of the Lord's saving work, will never fail. Physical healing, an outward expression of the deepest salvation, thus reveals the importance that man—in his entirety of soul and body—has for the Lord. Each sacrament, for that matter, expresses and actuates the closeness of God himself, who, in an absolutely freely-given way, "touches us through material things . . . that he takes up into his service, making them instruments of the encounter between us and himself" (*Homily*, Chrism Mass, 1 April 2010). "The unity between creation and redemption is made visible. The sacraments are an expression of the physicality of our faith, which embraces the whole person, body and soul" (*Homily*, Chrism Mass, 21 April 2011).

The principal task of the Church is certainly proclaiming the Kingdom of God, "But this very proclamation must be a process of healing: 'bind up the broken-hearted' (*Is* 61:1)" (*ibid.*), according to the charge entrusted by Jesus to his disciples (cf. *Lk* 9:1–2; *Mt* 10:1, 5–14; *Mk* 6:7–13). The tandem of physical health and renewal after lacerations of the soul thus helps us to understand better the "sacraments of healing." . . .

From a reading of the Gospels it emerges clearly that Jesus always showed special concern for sick people. He not only sent out his disciples to tend their wounds (cf. *Mt* 10:8; *Lk* 9:2; 10:9) but also instituted for them a specific sacrament: the Anointing of the Sick. The *Letter of James* attests to the presence of this sacramental act already in the first Christian community (cf. 5:14–16): by the Anointing of the Sick, accompanied by the prayer of the elders, the whole of the Church commends the sick to the suffering and glorified Lord so that he may alleviate their sufferings and save them; indeed she exhorts them to unite themselves spiritually to the passion and death of Christ so as to contribute thereby to the good of the People of God.

This sacrament leads us to contemplate the double mystery of the Mount of Olives, where Jesus found himself dramatically confronted by the path indicated to him by the Father, that of his Passion, the supreme act of love; and he accepted it. In that hour of tribulation, he is the mediator, "bearing in himself, taking upon himself the sufferings and passion of the world, transforming it into a cry to God, bringing it before the eyes and into the hands of God and thus truly bringing it to the moment of redemption" (*Lectio Divina*, Meeting with the Parish Priests of Rome, 18 February 2010). But "the Garden of Olives is also the place from which he ascended to the Father, and is therefore the place of redemption. . . . This double mystery of the Mount of Olives is also always 'at work' within the Church's sacramental oil . . . the sign of God's goodness reaching out to touch us" (*Homily*, Chrism Mass, 1 April 2010). In the Anointing of the Sick, the sacramental matter of the oil is offered to us, so to speak, "as God's medicine . . . which now assures us of his goodness, offering us strength and consolation, yet at the same time points beyond the moment of the illness towards the definitive healing, the resurrection (cf. *Jas* 5:14)" (*ibid.*).

This sacrament deserves greater consideration today both in theological reflection and in pastoral ministry among the sick. Through a proper appreciation of the content of the liturgical prayers that are adapted to the various human situations connected with illness, and not only when a person is at the end of his or her life (cf. *Catechism of the Catholic Church*, 1514), the Anointing of the Sick should not be held to be almost "a minor sacrament" when compared to the others. Attention to and pastoral care for sick people, while, on the one hand, a sign of God's tenderness towards those who are suffering, on the other brings spiritual advantage to priests and the whole Christian community as well, in the awareness that what is done to the least, is done to Jesus himself (cf. *Mt* 25:40).

QUESTIONS FOR REVIEW

1. How did the celebration of the Anointing of the Sick change after the Second Vatican Council?
2. What is Viaticum and when is it administered?
3. What are the effects of the Anointing of the Sick for those who are very ill?
4. What are the effects of the Anointing of the Sick for those who are dying?
5. How many times can you receive the Anointing of the Sick?

QUESTIONS FOR DISCUSSION

1. What are some of the temptations those who are gravely ill or injured can face?
2. How could the graces of the Anointing of the Sick help us face those temptations?

Part VII

Holy Orders

Thus far, all the sacraments that we have looked at have as their primary effect something concerned with an individual's personal salvation: Baptism washes away a person's sins; Confirmation seals a person with the Holy Spirit; the Eucharist unites a person with the Body and Blood of Jesus; Penance and Reconciliation forgive post-baptismal sin; and Anointing of the Sick heals a person from the remnants of sin while restoring the body according to the will of God.

That is not to say that each of these sacraments does not also have an ecclesial effect: Baptism makes a person a member of the Church; Confirmation gives a person an adult share in the mission of the Church; the Eucharist *makes* the Church; Penance and Reconciliation restore a person to fellowship with the Church; and Anointing of the Sick configures a person fully to the relationship with Jesus crucified at the heart of the Church.

The ecclesial effect of each of these sacraments, however, is a *consequence* of the personal effect: Baptism makes us a member of the Church *by* forgiving our sins; Confirmation gives us an adult share in the mission of the Church *by* sealing us with the Holy Spirit; the Eucharist makes the Church *by* uniting us with the Body and Blood of Jesus; Penance and Reconciliation restore us to fellowship with the Church *by* forgiving our post-baptismal sins; Anointing of the Sick configures us fully to the relationship at the heart of the Church *by* healing us from the remnants of sin and, where it is the will of God, healing us from bodily sickness.

That having been said, community is not merely a secondary consequence of what Christians do. Community is at the heart of the Christian life because the sacrificial worship of God that the Church undertakes is a communal act. From the day that God remarked, "It is not good that the man should be alone; I will make him a helper fit for him" (Gen 2:18), God called people to himself *together* so that they might worship him *together*.

> You never cease to gather a people to yourself, so that from the rising of the sun to its setting a pure sacrifice may be offered to your name.[1]

To live in community takes more than having one's personal needs satisfied. Living in community requires service to the community so as to sustain it and help it flourish. It is no different with the Church. As a community, the Church needs our service to sustain it and help it flourish.

Just as God gives us grace through the sacraments to nourish us and help us to grow personally, so also he gives us grace through the sacraments to help nourish and grow our community. There are two sacraments directed toward this goal: Holy Orders and Marriage. These sacraments are called the "Sacraments at the Service of Communion" because "[they] are directed towards the salvation of others; if they contribute as well to personal salvation, it is through service to others that they do so. They confer a particular mission in the Church and serve to build up the People of God" (CCC 1534). Holy Orders builds up the People of God by sanctifying the Church; Marriage builds up the People of God by sanctifying the world.

Holy Orders, or Ordination, is the sixth of the seven sacraments, as well as the first Sacrament at the Service of Communion. Its name comes from the Latin words *ordo* and *ordinatio*. *Ordo* refers to a "governing body" (CCC 1537), and *ordinatio* refers to the process by which a person was constituted as a member of such a body (CCC 1538). The Sacrament of Holy Orders is conferred in three degrees, which are received successively: the diaconate, the presbyterate, and the episcopate. In the central moment of Ordination, a bishop lays hands on a baptized and confirmed man and prays a prayer that consecrates that man, elevating him to the intended degree of Holy Orders (CCC 1538).

---

[1] Preface, Eucharistic Prayer III, in *The Roman Missal,* §108.

Chapter 1

Understanding the Sacrament

Old Testament

|| Assigned Reading
|| Exodus 28–32

When we were discussing the Eucharist, we saw how the Sacrifice of the Mass was prefigured in the sacrifices that people offered to God all throughout the Old Testament: the sacrifice of Abel, the sacrifices of Abraham, the sacrifice of Melchizedek, and the sacrifices of the people of Israel under the Mosaic Law. We have yet to discuss the people who offered those sacrifices. Those people were priests.

The basic definition of a priest is "one who offers sacrifice." From the beginning, humanity was called to priestly worship, and the context for that priestly worship was the family (Gen 4:3–4). Ordinarily, the patriarch of a family was its leader, its teacher, and its priest. This was true of Noah, who offered sacrifice to God from among the animals on the ark on behalf of his family (Gen 8:20). It was true of Melchizedek, the King of Salem, who offered a sacrifice of bread and wine (Gen 14:18–24). It was also true of Abraham, who offered sacrifice to God when God appeared to him (Gen 12:7; 13:4; 13:18; 22:13).

When God elevated his people to the status of a nation in the Mosaic Covenant, he instituted a national priesthood as part of the Mosaic Law and called the nation of Israel to the sacrificial worship of God through this priesthood (Exod 28–29). But he separated that priesthood from leading (kingship) and teaching (prophecy). The people called to the priesthood were Moses' brother Aaron and Aaron's male descendants (Exod 28:1). Aaron's direct successors later came to be called the "high priests." They wore special robes (Exod 28:2–3) and performed special sacrifices, like the yearly sacrifice on the Day of Atonement (Lev 16), which the other priests did not. Aaron's sons were consecrated with him as priests at Aaron's service (Exod 29). Their successors later came to be called "Aaronide priests." All of the priests were consecrated to God with the blood of a sacrificial ram and by being anointed with the Holy Anointing Oil—the same oil used to consecrate kings and prophets.

The Mosaic priests were not always faithful to their office. Shortly after his ordination to the priesthood, Aaron sinned against God by breaking the First Commandment: he fashioned a golden calf and led the Israelites in bowing down to it (Exod 32:1–6). When Moses discovered the sin, he looked to see who among the people of Israel were willing to repent; the first to rally to him was the Tribe of Levi, the "Levites," the tribe from which Aaron and his sons had come. Because of their swift repentance and their willingness to serve the Lord in keeping the people faithful to the Commandments, Moses welcomed them into a special service (Exod 32:25–29): they would be set aside for the service of the priests, although they themselves would not offer sacrifices (Num 3:5–13; 18:1–7).

Another time that the Mosaic priests were not faithful to their office was during the time of Samuel. At that time, two priests, Phinehas and Hophni, were abusing their office. They would abuse the sacrificial office by committing the sin of fornication with the women who served at the door and by stealing all the best food from the sacrificial animals, even if God had not set aside that food for the priests in the Mosaic Law (1 Sam 2:12–17, 22); furthermore, they disregarded their father's warning to stop their evil behavior (1 Sam 2:23–25). In response, God removed them from their priestly service. As we noted above when we were discussing Confirmation, God also promised to raise up a priest who was faithful to him forever (1 Sam 2:35), just like he promised to raise up a faithful prophet (Deut 18:18) and a faithful king (2 Sam 7:12).

New Testament

|| ASSIGNED READING
|| Hebrews 7–10

In our discussions of the other sacraments, we have already learned a significant amount about the priestly, sacrificial ministry to which Jesus called his disciples. When we were discussing the Sacrament of Confirmation, we saw that Jesus was the prophet, priest, and king that God promised, and that he poured out his Holy Spirit upon the Church at Pentecost to give its members a share in his prophetic, priestly, and royal offices (CCC 1544). When we were discussing the Sacrament of the Eucharist, we saw that Jesus specifically commanded his Church to continue the sacrificial worship of him by offering his Body and Blood. When we were discussing the Sacrament of Penance and Reconciliation, we saw that after the Resurrection Jesus breathed his Holy Spirit on his Apostles to give them the priestly power to forgive sins. When we were discussing the Sacrament of the Anointing of the Sick, we saw that this priestly power included the authority to heal people not only from sin but also from sickness, and to prepare them to go home to heaven and to be raised up on the last day.

The Acts of the Apostles describes three ways in which people are set aside to participate in the priestly office of Jesus through the sacrificial worship of him. The first and foremost of these is by being an Apostle. The word "apostle" comes from the Greek word *apostolos*, meaning "one who has been sent." The Apostles are those whom Jesus sent out when he breathed the Holy Spirit upon them to bestow upon them the office of priesthood. "As the Father has sent me, even so I send you" (John 20:21). Just as Jesus is a "priest for ever according to the order of Melchiz'edek" (Ps 110:4; Heb 7:17; CCC 1544), which is to say a prophet, priest, and king for his people, so likewise do the Apostles exercise a full share in Jesus' three offices: prophet, priest, and king. Like Peter on the day of Pentecost and James and John thereafter, they preach; like Paul in Ephesus, they sanctify; gathered together awaiting the Holy Spirit, they govern.

When the Apostles needed to pass on a complete sharing in their apostolic ministry, they laid hands upon a person and prayed over that person. This conferred upon that person a sharing in the Holy Spirit for the fulfillment of the apostolic office (Acts 13:3; 1 Tim 4:14; 2 Tim 1:6). These people were called "bishops." The Greek word for this is *episcopos*, from which we get the English word "episcopate," meaning "the office of bishop" (CCC 1555–1557).

Just as Aaron and his successors, the high priests, were not left alone in the Old Testament but were assisted in the sacrificial worship of God by the Aaronide priests, and just like the priests were not left alone but were ministered to by a group of faithful men called from among Israel not for sacrifice but for service, so also the Apostles and their successors in the episcopate have assistance from two other bodies of people.

The first of these are "presbyters." "Presbyter" comes from the Greek word *presbyteros*, meaning "elder." In Judaism at the time of Jesus, a *presbyteros* was a person who sat in council with the high priest on the body that governed the religious and political affairs of the Jews, the Sanhedrin; these people were originally Aaronide priests. The presbyters in the Acts of the Apostles are priests who sit in council with the bishops and assist them in teaching, sanctifying, and governing the Church (CCC 1562; Acts 15:2, 4, 6, 22, 23).

The second of these bodies that assist bishops are "deacons." "Deacon" comes from the Greek word *diakonos*, meaning "minister." Just as the Levites were ministers to the high priests and the Aaronide priests, so likewise did the Apostles have a need for men to serve them and to help them in the fulfillment of their apostolic duties, particularly that of charitable service. And just like the Levites were called out by Moses because of their faithfulness, so likewise did the Apostles choose "men of good repute, full of the Spirit and of wisdom" to ordain to the diaconate (Acts 6:3; CCC 1569). In order to constitute them as deacons, the Apostles "prayed and laid their hands upon them" (Acts 6:6), just as they did when they wanted to ordain someone to other offices of sacred ministry.

History and Theology

|| Assigned Reading
|| CCC 1536–1600

From apostolic times, the members of the Church recognized the importance of being united with the ordained ministers of the Church, especially in the sacrifice of the Eucharist. Writing around 100, Ignatius of Antioch exhorts all Christians always to stay faithful to their bishops, priests, and deacons in the sacrificial worship of Jesus:

> Let no man deceive himself: if anyone be not within the altar, he is deprived of the bread of God. For if the prayer of one or two possesses such power that Christ stands in the midst of them, how much more will the prayer of the bishop and of the whole Church, ascending up in harmony to God, prevail for the granting of all their petitions in Christ! He, therefore, that separates himself from such, and does not meet in the society where sacrifices are offered, and with "the Church of the first-born whose names are written in heaven" (Heb. 12:23), is a wolf in sheep's clothing, while he presents a mild outward appearance. Do ye, beloved, be careful to be subject to the bishop, and the presbyters and the deacons. For he that is subject to these is obedient to Christ, who has appointed them; but he that is disobedient to these is disobedient to Christ Jesus. And "he that obeys not the Son shall not see life, but the wrath of God abides on him" (John 3:36). For he that yields not obedience to his superiors is self-confident, quarrelsome, and proud. But "God," says [the Scripture] "resists the proud, but gives grace to the humble" (James 4:6); and, "The proud have greatly transgressed" (Psalm 119:51). The Lord also says to the priests, "He

that hears you, hears Me; and he that hears Me, hears the Father
that sent Me. He that despises you, despises Me; and he that
despises Me, despises Him that sent Me" (see Luke 10:16; John
12:49–50).[1]

At the local level, one way we can be sure that we are staying in union
with Jesus is to make sure that we are listening to the bishops, priests,
and deacons of the Catholic Church, receiving the sacraments from
them, and being obedient to them. This is the surest way to stay faithful to Jesus Christ, who called them into his ordained ministry and who
teaches, sanctifies, and governs us through them. However, there are also
bishops, priests, and deacons (or people who use those titles) outside
of the Catholic Church, and so it can be confusing sometimes to figure
out through whom Jesus intends to teach, sanctify, and govern us. This
was already an issue in the early Church—people went around claiming
to be sent by Christ, when in fact what they were teaching, doing, and
commanding were contrary to the will of Christ.

> I am astonished that you are so quickly deserting him who called
> you in the grace of Christ and turning to a different gospel—not
> that there is another gospel, but there are some who trouble you
> and want to pervert the gospel of Christ. But even if we, or an
> angel from heaven, should preach to you a gospel contrary to
> that which we preached to you, let him be accursed. As we have
> said before, so now I say again, If any one is preaching to you a
> gospel contrary to that which you received, let him be accursed.
> (Gal 1:6–9)

St. Paul warns us not to be led astray by those who claim to speak for
Christ but don't. How, then, can we tell the difference?

In the Gospel, Jesus raises all the Apostles to a full share in his prophetic, priestly, and royal offices. But among the Apostles, Jesus chose
one, Peter, for a special ministry to the rest. When Peter confessed

---

[1]   Ignatius of Antioch, *Letter to the Ephesians* 5 (ANF 1:51).

that Jesus was the Messiah, Jesus gave him the "keys of the kingdom of heaven" (Matt 16:19). Those keys were a symbol of authority. In the Old Testament, the keys to a kingdom were possessed by an "over the house official," also called a "master of the sacred palace," to whom the king delegated his royal authority (Gen 41:37–43; Isa 22:15–25). That royal official possessed the fullness of the king's authority. His commands were the king's commands; his prohibitions were the king's prohibitions.

In the early Church, Peter occupied a special office among the other Apostles. Even though he was an Apostle like them, he had been constituted the "over the house official" of God's kingdom in a way that they had not. When a new Apostle needed to be appointed, it was Peter who led the decision-making (Acts 1:15). When the Holy Spirit came down upon the Church, it was Peter who preached the Gospel (Acts 2:14). When all the Apostles and their presbyters met in council, it was Peter who first spoke what was to be their decision (Acts 15:7–11).

Throughout the history of the Church, Peter and his successors, the bishops of Rome, have occupied a special place among the other bishops. Looking for the surest and quickest way to give others a guide to right belief, Irenaeus of Lyon in the second century looked to Rome:

Since, however, it would be very tedious, in such a volume as this, to reckon up the successions of all the Churches, we do put to confusion all those who, in whatever manner, whether by an evil self-pleasing, by vainglory, or by blindness and perverse opinion, assemble in unauthorized meetings; [we do this, I say,] by indicating that tradition derived from the apostles, of the very great, the very ancient, and universally known Church founded and organized at Rome by the two most glorious apostles, Peter and Paul; as also [by pointing out] the faith preached to men, which comes down to our time by means of the successions of the bishops. For it is a matter of necessity that every Church should agree with this Church, on account of its preeminent authority, that is, the faithful everywhere, inasmuch as the tradition has been preserved continuously by those [faithful men] who exist everywhere.[2]

Irenaeus then goes on to recount how, in an unbroken chain of successors (starting with Peter, continuing to Linus, then to Clement, and so on and so forth), the bishops of Rome have preserved unbroken the doctrine of Christ and intervened when necessary to keep the Church in other locations faithful to Christ's teaching, worship, and commandments.[3] In this way, Irenaeus helped the Church to understand the significance of papal primacy: only those bishops, priests, and deacons in union with the pope, the bishop of Rome, speak for and are sent directly by Christ.

The Second Vatican Council summarized the relationship between the successors of Peter and the other bishops. All bishops, in virtue of their ordination, possess the fullness of power to teach, sanctify, and govern the Church in the name of Christ (CCC 1558);[4] they all have a solicitude for the whole Church (CCC 1560).[5]

But the college or body of bishops has no authority unless it is understood together with the Roman Pontiff, the successor of Peter as its head. The pope's power of primacy over all, both pastors and faithful, remains whole and intact. In virtue of his office, that is as Vicar of Christ and pastor of the whole Church, the Roman Pontiff has full, supreme and universal power over the Church. And he is always free to exercise this power. The order of bishops, which succeeds to the college of apostles and gives this apostolic body continued existence, is also the subject of supreme and full power over the universal Church, provided we understand this body together with its head the Roman Pontiff and never without this head. This power can be exercised only with the consent of the Roman Pontiff. For our Lord

---

[2]   Irenaeus of Lyon, *Adversus Haereses* 3.3.2 (ANF 1:415–416).
[3]   Irenaeus of Lyon, *Adversus Haereses* 3.3.3 (ANF 1:416).
[4]   Second Vatican Council, *Lumen Gentium*, §21.
[5]   Second Vatican Council, *Lumen Gentium*, §23.

placed Simon alone as the rock and the bearer of the keys of the Church, and made him shepherd of the whole flock; it is evident, however, that the power of binding and loosing, which was given to Peter, was granted also to the college of apostles, joined with their head. This college, insofar as it is composed of many, expresses the variety and universality of the People of God, but insofar as it is assembled under one head, it expresses the unity of the flock of Christ.[6]

The papacy is not a sacrament; in that sense, the pope is a bishop among other bishops. But the papacy is a special office, instituted by Christ and given to Peter and his successors. In that sense, *this* bishop, the bishop of Rome, is the very focal point of the unity of all who legitimately exercise their ordained ministry, whether bishops, priests, or deacons.

QUESTIONS FOR REVIEW

1. What is the most basic function of any priest, Catholic or not?
2. What priesthood did God establish in the Old Testament? Who could be priests?
3. What are the three different ways that men can be sacramentally ordained to participate in Jesus' priesthood? Name and define each.
4. What special task did Jesus entrust to Peter?
5. Who carries on that task today?

QUESTIONS FOR DISCUSSION

1. Have you ever known a priest who brought Jesus especially close to you? How could you see Jesus working through him?
2. How much do you know about our present pope? How does he inspire you or challenge you?

---

[6] Second Vatican Council, *Lumen Gentium*, §22.

Chapter 2

LIVING THE SACRAMENT

|| Assigned Reading
|| CIC, Canons 1010–1054

Celebration

What is necessary for Ordination to one of the three degrees of Holy Orders happens at the central moment of the celebration: a bishop lays hands upon a baptized man and prays a prayer consecrating him for service in the relevant degree of Holy Orders by calling forth the Holy Spirit (CCC 1573, 1024; CIC, Canon 1009, §2; 1012). The candidate receives that outpouring of the Holy Spirit, which confers on him a sacramental character, like that of Baptism and Confirmation. That character empowers him for service in the specified degree of Holy Orders (CCC 1581–1582; CIC, Canon 1008).

The minister of the Sacrament of Holy Orders is always a bishop. An ancient saying in philosophy tells us that "no one gives what he does not have." Since the conferral of Holy Orders involves a pouring out of the Holy Spirit for a ministerial share in Christ's prophetic, priestly, and kingly offices (CCC 1585), and since only the Apostles received the Holy Spirit from Christ for this purpose, only their successors, the bishops, are capable of conferring that share in the Holy Spirit (CCC 1575–1576). Of himself, one bishop has the power to confer Holy Orders to any degree.

Nevertheless, in order to ensure that there is no room for error in epis-copal Ordinations and to encourage collegiality among the bishops, it is required that two bishops assist the principal consecrator when ordain-ing a new bishop; indeed all bishops present at an episcopal Ordination are welcome to participate (CIC, Canon 1014).

Only men can be candidates for Holy Orders. Christ himself is so visibly present in his ordained ministers (CCC 1548–1549), in fulfill-ment of the ministry exercised by the patriarchs and entrusted to Aaron, his sons, and the sons of Levi, that the reservation of the Sacrament of Holy Orders to men is not a matter of preference; it is a matter of unchangeable doctrine, consistent with God's choices throughout the whole of salvation history:

> The Lord Jesus chose men (*viri*) to form the college of the twelve apostles, and the apostles did the same when they chose collab-orators to succeed them in their ministry [Cf. *Mk* 3:14–19; *Lk* 6:12–16; *1 Tim* 3:1–13; *2 Tim* 1:6; *Titus* 1:5–9; St. Clement of Rome, *Ad Cor.* 42, 4; 44, 3: PG 1, 292–293; 300]. The college of bishops, with whom the priests are united in the priesthood, makes the college of the twelve an ever-present and ever-active reality until Christ's return. The Church recognizes herself to be bound by this choice made by the Lord himself. For this reason the ordination of women is not possible [Cf. John Paul II, MD 26–27; CDF, declaration, *Inter insigniores*: AAS 69 (1977) 98–116]. (CCC 1577)

Men who are going to be ordained must first be baptized (CCC 1577; CIC, Canon 1024). That is because they must be first made members of the Church over which they are to exercise Christ's prophetic, priestly, and kingly offices. They should also be confirmed before being ordained, so as to be empowered for public witness before being placed in public responsibility (CIC, Canon 1033). As was the case with the Levites, the Apostles, and the first men that the Apostles called into ordained minis-try with them, candidates for Ordination should also be men of exem-plary faith, life, prayer, and virtue (CIC, Canon 1029).

In the Latin Rite, with the exception of the permanent deacons who are never going to be ordained priests, the Church has observed the discipline of exclusive celibacy among those in Holy Orders for the last thousand years, universalizing a widespread custom that had been in existence among the clergy since time immemorial (CCC 1579; CIC, Canon 1037). The tradition follows counsel that Jesus himself gave to his Apostles (Matt 19:10–12). In the Eastern Rites, married men are permitted to be ordained deacons and priests, but not bishops; all the same, no man may marry after he has been ordained (CCC 1580).

Since those who possess Holy Orders possess the most complete sharing in the prophetic, priestly, and kingly offices of Christ that is possible in this life, there are a variety of liturgical rites surrounding the central moment of Ordination. These rites prepare the men who are to be ordained to receive their ordination and add to the symbolism of what they receive through the laying on of hands (CCC 1574). In the Latin Rite, there are four acts that precede Ordination.

First, the candidates for Ordination are presented to the bishop and chosen by him. At the moment when the bishop chooses them, the Church publicly confirms that what the candidates have experienced as God's call to Holy Orders is in fact a genuine vocation.

No one has a *right* to receive the sacrament of Holy Orders. Indeed no one claims this office for himself; he is called to it by God [Cf. *Heb* 5:4]. Anyone who thinks he recognizes the signs of God's call to the ordained ministry must humbly submit his desire to the authority of the Church, who has the responsibility and right to call someone to receive orders. Like every grace this sacrament can be *received* only as an unmerited gift. (CCC 1578)

After the candidates are chosen, the bishop instructs them in their responsibility. No one can be forced into Holy Orders (CIC, Canon 1026), and so the Church desires that those to be ordained are fully conscious of the nature and responsibility of the degree of Holy Orders they are to receive.

After the candidates are instructed, the whole Church prays the Litany of the Saints over them. This calls down the grace of God upon the candidates, reminds all present that it is only by grace that anyone faithfully fulfills the office, and unites the Church on earth with the Church in heaven, including the many saintly ordained men who have passed from this life to the next.

Only after being presented, chosen, instructed, and prepared through prayer are the candidates for Ordination actually ordained. When the bishop lays hands on them and prays the prayer of consecration—a prayer prefaced by recalling the connection of that order with high priests, priests, or Levites, as appropriate (CCC 1541–1543)—they receive the Sacrament of Holy Orders.

Immediately following their ordination, other rites are performed to complete the symbolism of the event. Since priests will, with their hands, offer the sacrifice of Jesus' Body and Blood, and since bishops will additionally, with their hands, raise others to Holy Orders, those who are ordained priests or bishops receive an anointing and consecration of their hands with sacred chrism oil. Lastly, the Church completes the significance of the event by

> giving the book of the Gospels, the ring, the miter, and the crosier to the bishop as the sign of his apostolic mission to proclaim the Word of God, of his fidelity to the Church, the bride of Christ, and his office as shepherd of the Lord's flock; [the] presentation to the priest of the paten and chalice, "the offering of the holy people" which he is called to present to God; giving the book of the Gospels to the deacon who has just received the mission to proclaim the Gospel of Christ. (CCC 1574)

Having received the insignia of their office, the newly ordained men exchange the kiss of peace with the bishop as a sign of being welcomed into the body, or *ordo*, to which he has ordained them. There follows the Sacrifice of the Mass, in which all the ordained of whatever rank, together with the laity, renew their devotion to the one sacrifice of Christ which is the ground of all priestly service and sacrifice (CCC 1544–1545).

Effects of the Sacrament

"The grace of the Holy Spirit proper to this sacrament is configuration to Christ as Priest, Teacher, and Pastor, of whom the ordained is made a minister" (CCC 1585), and a strengthening for the office to which a person has been ordained (CCC 1586–1588). The principal effect of that grace is the conferral of an indelible character (CCC 1581). This character, like that of Baptism and Confirmation, confers new power upon the person who receives it and is permanent such that it can never be lost or repeated. Even in the case of priests or other ordained ministers who desire or are asked to leave active ministry, they can never lose Ordination; since it is indelible, they can only refrain from practicing what they can never lose (CCC 1583).

The diaconate is the first degree of Holy Orders. Those who are ordained deacons receive a character which configures them to Christ the *"servant* of all" (CCC 1570). They participate in Christ's royal office by becoming leaders in service, especially charitable ministries. They participate in Christ's priestly office by serving bishops and priests in the celebration of the sacraments, especially the Mass. They participate in Christ's prophetic office by proclaiming the Gospel.

The presbyterate is the second degree of Holy Orders. Those who are ordained priests receive a character that configures them to Christ the priest (CCC 1563). This character enables them to act *in persona Christi capitis* (in the person of Christ, the head of the Church), although they do so always as collaborators with the bishop and depending "on the bishops in the exercise of their own proper power" (CCC 1564). As priests, their proper ministry and the primary means by which they participate in Christ's priestly office is the celebration of the Sacrifice of the Mass (CCC 1566). Priests also participate in Christ's priestly office when they celebrate the other sacraments that they are capable of celebrating: Baptism, Confirmation, Penance and Reconciliation, and Anointing of the Sick. They participate in Christ's prophetic office by preaching. They participate in Christ's royal office by governing what may have been entrusted to them; this is especially the case when they are made the pastors of parishes.

The episcopate is the third degree of Holy Orders. Those who are ordained bishops receive a character that enables them to act as Christ's representative and to take a complete share in Christ's prophetic, priestly, and kingly offices. Where deacons *proclaim* and priests *preach*, bishops possess by their episcopal character the power to *teach* with magisterial authority; where deacons assist and priests depend on the bishop for the exercise of their proper power, bishops possess in themselves the power to celebrate the sacraments without any other delegation; where deacons lead in service and priests govern only in what has been entrusted to them by bishops, bishops possess the power and authority to govern a diocese.

Any time that an ordained minister exercises his ordained ministry, he acts as an instrument of Christ. As such, he ought to exercise his power in the manner that Christ wills: as a servant (CCC 1551). Nevertheless, Holy Orders does not in any way remove a person's free will. Bishops, priests, and deacons are subject to all the same temptations to sin as other Christians. When they sin, however, this does not take away the efficacy of their sacramental ministry, because their ministry is rooted in a sacramental character. Just like when we sin we can still receive the Sacrament of Penance and Reconciliation because we have not lost the character of our Baptism, so likewise when men in Holy Orders sin, they still proclaim, preach, and teach the words of Christ; they still celebrate the sacraments of Christ; they still govern the Church of Christ. The power of the Holy Spirit guarantees that they can still exercise these ministries even if the fruitfulness of their doing so might be tarnished if they do not live up to the standards that Christ set (CCC 1550). However worthy or unworthy an individual man might be, Christ does not ever cease to provide sacramental ministry to his Church (CCC 1584). This is part of God's providential plan and a great source of comfort to Christians. God never ceases to provide for the needs of the Church.[1]

---

[1] Aquinas, ST IIIa, q. 63, a. 3.

Appropriating and Living This Sacrament

The presence of ordained ministry in the Church does not in any way conflict with the share in Christ's prophetic, priestly, and royal offices that the laity possess in virtue of the Sacraments of Baptism and Confirmation; rather, it enables and empowers the laity. Let us recall that "the Church produces the Eucharist, but the Eucharist also produces the Church."[2] The ordained ministers of the Church provide for the sacramental needs of the Church, but in so doing they empower the members of the Church to live out their own Christian lives to the fullest.

The first and best way for the laity to live out the Sacrament of Holy Orders is to accept it from God with gratitude as a gift: to receive joyfully and in faith the proclamation, preaching, and teaching of God's ordained ministers; to receive frequently and in love the sacraments of God's ordained ministers; and to receive attentively and in obedience the governance of God's ordained ministers (Heb 13:17; 1 Thess 5:12–13). In so doing, the laity are empowered to live out the calling of their Baptism and their Confirmation, contribute to the good of the Church, and are empowered to live out their own Christian lives to the fullest.

The second way in which the laity can live out the Sacrament of Holy Orders is to support their ordained ministers. This happens in two ways. First and foremost, it happens with prayer. Mindful of the fact that the leaders of the Church are often subject to greater spiritual struggles than others (Eph 6:12), the laity can support those in Holy Orders by praying for them personally and for the fruitfulness of their ministry. Secondly, it happens with material support. St. Paul speaks at length about this obligation:

> Do you not know that those who are employed in the temple service get their food from the temple, and those who serve at the altar share in the sacrificial offerings? In the same way, the

---

[2] Henri de Lubac, *The Splendor of the Church*, trans. Michael Mason (San Francisco: Ignatius Press, 1999), 133.

Lord commanded that those who proclaim the gospel should get their living by the gospel. (1 Cor 9:13–14)

The Church explicitly acknowledges this obligation in canon law (CIC, Canon 222, §1). Although the Church does not tell us how much we should contribute to the material needs of the ordained, and Jesus does not require that one forsake one's legitimate familial obligations for the sake of an unattainable goal (Mark 7:9–13), a good goal has traditionally been understood to be the biblical tithe of ten percent.[3]

Finally, the laity can live out the Sacrament of Holy Orders by praying to God to call more people to the ordained ministry and by supporting people they know who are trying to answer a vocation faithfully. Jesus instructed his disciples to pray for vocations (Matt 9:38; Luke 10:2). Thomas Aquinas explains why:

By his liberality, God offers us many things even though we do not request them. Still, he wants to offer us some things in response to our requests, so that we build confidence in having recourse to God, and so that we recognize him as the author of our goods.[4]

God can give the Church all the ordained ministers it needs without our prayers and he often does. But as we have seen, God never wants to keep his good gifts to himself; he wants to share them with us. Even if he has called only some people to ordained ministry, he still wants us all to be participants in their call and in their faithful response. Thus, even if it is the bishop who confers the Sacrament of Holy Orders at the central moment of the celebration, all of the faithful who pray for vocations have a hand in bringing men to that moment and thereby providing for the spiritual needs of the Church.

---

[3] DH 797.
[4] Aquinas, ST IIa–IIae, q. 83, a. 2, ad 3 (Leonine 9:194).

SELECTED READING
Second Vatican Council, Dogmatic Constitution on the
Church *Lumen Gentium* (November 21, 1964), no. 28

Christ, whom the Father has sanctified and sent into the world, has
through His apostles, made their successors, the bishops, partakers of His consecration and His mission. They have legitimately
handed on to different individuals in the Church various degrees of
participation in this ministry. Thus the divinely established ecclesiastical ministry is exercised on different levels by those who from
antiquity have been called bishops, priests and deacons. Priests,
although they do not possess the highest degree of the priesthood,
and although they are dependent on the bishops in the exercise of
their power, nevertheless they are united with the bishops in sacerdotal dignity. By the power of the sacrament of Orders, in the image
of Christ the eternal high Priest, they are consecrated to preach the
Gospel and shepherd the faithful and to celebrate divine worship,
so that they are true priests of the New Testament. Partakers of the
function of Christ the sole Mediator, on their level of ministry, they
announce the divine word to all. They exercise their sacred function especially in the Eucharistic worship or the celebration of the
Mass by which acting in the person of Christ and proclaiming His
Mystery they unite the prayers of the faithful with the sacrifice of
their Head and renew and apply in the sacrifice of the Mass until the
coming of the Lord the only sacrifice of the New Testament namely
that of Christ offering Himself once for all a spotless Victim to the
Father. For the sick and the sinners among the faithful, they exercise
the ministry of alleviation and reconciliation and they present the
needs and the prayers of the faithful to God the Father. Exercising
within the limits of their authority the function of Christ as Shepherd and Head, they gather together God's family as a brotherhood
all of one mind, and lead them in the Spirit, through Christ, to God
the Father. In the midst of the flock they adore Him in spirit and in
truth. Finally, they labor in word and doctrine, believing what they
have read and meditated upon in the law of God, teaching what they

have believed, and putting in practice in their own lives what they have taught.

Priests, prudent cooperators with the Episcopal order, its aid and instrument, called to serve the people of God, constitute one priesthood with their bishop although bound by a diversity of duties. Associated with their bishop in a spirit of trust and generosity, they make him present in a certain sense in the individual local congregations, and take upon themselves, as far as they are able, his duties and the burden of his care, and discharge them with a daily interest. And as they sanctify and govern under the bishop's authority, that part of the Lord's flock entrusted to them they make the universal Church visible in their own locality and bring an efficacious assistance to the building up of the whole body of Christ. Intent always upon the welfare of God's children, they must strive to lend their effort to the pastoral work of the whole diocese, and even of the entire Church. On account of this sharing in their priesthood and mission, let priests sincerely look upon the bishop as their father and reverently obey him. And let the bishop regard his priests as his co-workers and as sons and friends, just as Christ called His disciples now not servants but friends. All priests, both diocesan and religious, by reason of Orders and ministry, fit into this body of bishops and priests, and serve the good of the whole Church according to their vocation and the grace given to them.

In virtue of their common sacred ordination and mission, all priests are bound together in intimate brotherhood, which naturally and freely manifests itself in mutual aid, spiritual as well as material, pastoral as well as personal, in their meetings and in communion of life, of labor and charity.

Let them, as fathers in Christ, take care of the faithful whom they have begotten by baptism and their teaching. Becoming from the heart a pattern to the flock, let them so lead and serve their local community that it may worthily be called by that name, by which the one and entire people of God is signed, namely, the Church of God. Let them remember that by their daily life and interests they are showing the face of a truly sacerdotal and pastoral ministry to the faithful and the infidel, to Catholics and non-Catholics, and that to all they bear witness to the truth and life, and as good shepherds go after those also, who though baptized in the Catholic Church have fallen away from the use of the sacraments, or even from the faith.

Because the human race today is joining more and more into a civic, economic and social unity, it is that much the more necessary that priests, by combined effort and aid, under the leadership of the bishops and the Supreme Pontiff, wipe out every kind of separateness, so that the whole human race may be brought into the unity of the family of God.

QUESTIONS FOR REVIEW

1. What gesture is central to the ordination of a priest?
2. Who is the minister of the Sacrament of Holy Orders and has the authority to ordain a priest?
3. How is Holy Orders like Baptism and Confirmation?
4. Does the personal holiness of a priest or bishop affect his ability to baptize, celebrate the Eucharist, forgive sins, or confect any other sacrament?
5. What guarantees the priest's ability to carry out his sacramental ministry?

QUESTIONS FOR DISCUSSION

1. What are some ways in which you and your family could work together to support those who serve you in sacramental ministry with your prayer, service, and generosity?
2. If you are a young man, have you ever prayed about a vocation to the priesthood? Why or why not? What are some ways we can support and encourage those who might be called to this vocation?

Part VIII

HOLY MATRIMONY

Marriage is the seventh of the seven sacraments and the second Sacrament at the Service of Communion. In the central moment of marriage, a baptized man and a baptized woman freely consent to enter into a lifelong, exclusive partnership ordered toward their good and the procreation and education of children (CCC 1601; CIC, Canon 1055). After they consummate this union by performing "between themselves in a human fashion a conjugal act which is suitable in itself for the procreation of offspring" (CIC, Canon 1061, §1), Christ makes their bond absolutely and altogether indissoluble save only by the death of one of the spouses (CCC 1640).

Chapter 1

Understanding the Sacrament

Old Testament

> **Assigned Reading**
> Genesis 2:18–25
> Hosea 1–2

For each of the other six sacraments, there were signs in the Old Testament that *pointed to* what Christ was going to institute in the New Testament, but did not *make happen* any portion of what Christ was going to institute for the Church. For those sacraments, we say that Jesus "instituted" them when he gave to the Church a sign that made things happen to replace the signs that did not. Marriage is different. Marriage did exist prior to the New Testament in a form that *made something happen*: a stable union between a man and a woman. When Jesus came, we do not say that he *instituted* marriage, because marriage was already there; rather, we say that he "raised marriage to the dignity of a sacrament," because he took the same actions that brought about a stable union between a man and a woman and, when they are performed between two people who are baptized, enriched them with the grace to make that union indissoluble (CCC 1601; CIC, Canon 1055, §2).

Initially, when God made the human race he made only one person, Adam (Gen 2:7). He placed Adam in the Garden of Eden with the job of tilling and keeping it (Gen 2:15). Of himself, Adam could only keep a small portion of the Garden. But God had bigger plans in mind for the human race. He wanted them to "Be fruitful and multiply, and fill the earth and subdue it" (Gen 1:28). This is to say that God had a very *Catholic* intention for humanity. The human family was to grow, to spread, and so to bring the worship of God to the ends of the earth as a domestic Church. Without a corresponding female companion and partner, Adam could not fulfill this goal.

Together, though, Adam and Eve could fulfill God's plan; in their mutual love, their mutual harmony, and mutual assistance, they could bring forth children in a relationship with God and begin the evangelization of the whole earth by the spread of their domestic church.

Sin disrupted that plan. Not only did it break the harmony between the human soul and God, causing spiritual death—as well as the harmony between the human body and the human soul, causing sickness and physical death—it also broke the harmony between human persons. Eve broke that harmony by tempting Adam into sin (Gen 3:6); Adam broke that harmony by blaming Eve for his own bad choice (Gen 3:12). That did not destroy the relationship between them any more than it destroyed human nature, but it did wound their relationship just like it wounded human nature.

Adam and Eve would go on to have children (Gen 4:1–2, 25), and from those children all the families of the earth recounted in the Scriptures would be born (Gen 5 and 10). Only now, the children would be born outside a relationship with God because of original sin and would have to be brought back into a relationship with God through the Sacrament of Baptism. Adam and Eve, together with their children, could be fruitful and multiply and could fill the earth and subdue it, but since they would now do so outside the domestic church that God planned for them, their mission would be tainted by the desire for domination rather than service (Gen 3:16), by toil rather than by satisfaction (Gen 3:17–19).

When we discussed the Sacrament of the Anointing of the Sick, we saw how part of God's plan to heal humanity from the effects of sin was his healing of women who suffered from infertility: Sarah, Rachel, the wife of Zorah, Hannah, and Elizabeth. These healings restored the brokenness of marriage by restoring something of God's original blessing. It was not the act of bearing children that restored blessing to these mothers *per se*; rather, it was the act of bringing forth specific children—Isaac, Joseph, Samson, Samuel, and John the Baptist: children who would prepare the way for and foreshadow Jesus Christ, the Savior of the human race. In so doing, these women prepared ultimately for the restoration of all the blessings that God had in store for humanity, when, in the person of Jesus Christ, God came down to earth and empowered his disciples to fulfill God's original, Catholic intention for humanity: "And Jesus came and said to them, 'All authority in heaven and on earth has been given to me. Go therefore and make disciples of all nations, baptizing them in the name of the Father and of the Son and of the Holy Spirit, teaching them to observe all that I have commanded you; and behold, I am with you always, to the close of the age'" (Matt 28:18–20).

In between the Fall and the coming of Jesus, marriage had a long way to go until it was restored to God's original purpose. So far had it fallen from God's plan that sometimes it would end in the separation of the spouses:

> When a man takes a wife and marries her, if then she finds no favor in his eyes because he has found some indecency in her, and he writes her a bill of divorce and puts it in her hand and sends her out of his house, and she departs out of his house, and if she goes and becomes another man's wife, and the latter husband dislikes her and writes her a bill of divorce and puts it in her hand and sends her out of his house, or if the latter husband dies, who took her to be his wife, then her former husband, who sent her away, may not take her again to be his wife, after she has been defiled; for that is an abomination before the LORD, and you shall not bring guilt upon the land which the LORD your God gives you for an inheritance. (Deut 24:1–4)

We have to be very careful with this text from the Mosaic Law. Notice that it never actually says, "you *should* get divorced," or even, "you *can* get divorced." Here's how the logic of the passage breaks down:

First, we have a situation:

- *when* a man takes a wife and marries her

Second, we have a long condition:

- *if* then she finds no favour
- *if* she goes and becomes another man's wife
  - *and* the latter husband sends her out
  - or *if* the latter husband dies

Only at the very end of the passage do we get an actual command:

- *then* her former husband may not take her again after she has been defiled

When someone gives a command in the form of a conditional statement, they don't command what comes after the *if*; they only command what comes after the *then*. If your teacher says to you, "If you cheat on a test, then you should not hide it," would you say that your teacher had commanded you to cheat? If your priest says to you, "If you sin, then you should go to Confession," would you say that your priest had commanded you to sin? In the passage from Deuteronomy, the only command given after the *then* concerns what a man who has sent his wife away may subsequently do to her. The text never commands him to put her away in the first place. In fact, the text assumes as a matter of course that, when a woman has been put away, a subsequent remarriage defiles her. The only thing that the text commands is that the man not take her back again because she has been defiled, a point which Jesus will take up in the Gospels, as we shall see below. Deuteronomy does not, therefore, command divorce. It acknowledges the regular occurrence of a very broken scenario that is not in accord with God's original intention for humanity and only commands men not to make a broken situation worse.

Needless to say, this passage from Deuteronomy was misunderstood over the course of the history of the people of Israel. Even though divorce comes after the *if* and not the *then*, it was understood by many Israelites to sanction divorce and to set forth the rules under which a man could divorce his wife. This caused a grave difficulty in the spiritual lives of the people of Israel before the coming of Jesus. Since God intended marriage to be a permanent union between a man and a woman, God often used marriage to represent his never-ending fidelity to the people he had chosen. But in a culture that came to recognize divorce, people could rightly wonder: If Israel had been unfaithful to God by its sins, especially the sin of idolatry, would it ever "find no favor" in God's eyes? Would God ever send the people of Israel out of his house into the house of other gods?

Already in the Old Testament, God intimated that he had no intention of forsaking the people he had chosen, however great their infidelity toward him may have been. In the Song of Songs, he signaled that he was awaiting the day patiently when he might be ultimately and finally united with them in a covenant with a permanency and exclusivity patterned on that of marriage as it had been intended from the beginning. Even when God called out the sins of Israel in the most striking of terms, likening the nation to a prostitute for going after other gods (Hos 1:2), he promised that he would remain a faithful spouse in the face of Israel's unfaithfulness: "I will espouse you for ever; I will espouse you in righteousness and in justice, in steadfast love, and in mercy. I will espouse you in faithfulness; and you shall know the LORD" (Hos 2:19–20).

The prophets describe such a marriage between God and Israel analogously with the miraculous births of Sarah, Rachel, the wife of Zorah, Hannah, and Elizabeth. To Isaiah, for example, Israel is like a barren wife. When she went astray to other gods, she became spiritually unfruitful because she became unable to fulfill God's Catholic intention for humanity. But the Lord, who made her, also promises to restore her fruitfulness.

Sing, O barren one, who did not bear;
    break forth into singing and cry aloud,
    you who have not had labor pains!
For the children of the desolate one will be more
    than the children of her that is married, says the LORD.
Enlarge the place of your tent,
    and let the curtains of your habitations be stretched out;
hold not back, lengthen your cords
    and strengthen your stakes.
For you will spread abroad to the right and to the left,
    and your descendants will possess the nations
    and will people the desolate cities.

Fear not, for you will not be ashamed;
    be not confounded, for you will not be put to shame;
for you will forget the shame of your youth,
    and the reproach of your widowhood you will remember
        no more.
For your Maker is your husband,
    the LORD of hosts is his name;
and the Holy One of Israel is your Redeemer,
    the God of the whole earth he is called. (Isa 54:1–5)

New Testament

|| **ASSIGNED READING**
|| John 2:1–12

In the New Testament, Jesus raises marriage to the dignity of a sacrament by making it *point to* and *cause* his love for the Church. He does this by his presence at the Wedding Feast at Cana (John 2:1–12). In the Ancient Near East, wedding feasts were a big deal—even bigger than they are today. Rather than lasting a few hours, like a typical American wedding reception, they lasted for a whole week. During that time, the bridegroom's parents were expected to provide enough wine for everyone to drink. To run out would have been an embarrassing failure, and that is precisely what happened at this wedding feast.

The wedding feast was symbolic of the relationship between God and the people of Israel. He espoused them as a nation on Mount Sinai when he established the Mosaic Covenant with them. But the celebration was cut short by the worship of the golden calf and the subsequent sins that Israel committed against God. The question that remained for the people, as we saw in the previous chapter, was whether God would remain faithful in spite of Israel's infidelity, or whether God would put her out of his house like one of the men mentioned in Deuteronomy 24.

At Cana, Mary intercedes with Jesus to act definitively (John 2:3). At her request, Jesus, the bridegroom of the people of Israel, steps in and saves the bride's family from embarrassment. He turns massive jars of water into the best wine the people had ever tasted. (About 750 bottles' worth by contemporary standards!) In this way, Jesus made the wedding feast at Cana a sign that *pointed to* his love for the Church. When the people of Israel, his bride, failed to remain faithful to him, he stepped in and made up for what they lacked by offering himself on the Cross. His suffering on the Cross not only made up for their sins and the sins of all humanity against him, it showered down upon the whole of humanity a superabundance of love like the superabundance of wine that he made at the wedding feast of Cana.

Jesus' actions at Cana illuminate what he says elsewhere about divorce. Let us recall that Deuteronomy never commanded divorce. Divorce followed the *if*, not the *then*. Deuteronomy observed that remarriage after divorce defiles a woman; the only thing that Deuteronomy commanded was that a man not take back his wife after she had been defiled. Jesus' actions at Cana show that he has no intention of divorcing Israel. His words at the Sermon on the Mount, which are echoed in all of the Synoptic Gospels, confirm this:

> It was also said, "Whoever divorces his wife, let him give her a certificate of divorce." But I say to you that every one who divorces

his wife, except on the ground of unchastity, makes her an adulteress; and whoever marries a divorced woman commits adultery. (Matt 5:31–32; see Matt 19:9; Luke 16:18; Mark 10:11–12)

Let's be very careful about what Jesus says here. If your mother says to you, "Whoever teases her brother, unless he was already angry, is responsible for him getting angry," does that mean that your mother permits you to tease your brother if he gets angry at you? Or if your teacher says, "Whoever looks the other way while a friend copies his homework, unless the friend was already copying someone else's homework, makes him into a cheater," does that mean your teacher permits you to let people copy your homework? Of course not. It's the same with Jesus. Jesus says that if a man divorces his wife, he makes her an adulteress, because the presumption is that she will go and marry someone else. The one exception to the rule is if she was already committing adultery. In that case, the man can't make her an adulteress because she has already made herself one. Either way, Jesus condemns remarriage to someone whose first spouse is still living as adultery. Deuteronomy said that remarriage defiles a woman. Jesus says the same thing, but from the perspective of the man: "whoever marries a divorced woman commits adultery" (Matt 5:32).

The New Testament presents Jesus' teaching about marriage as a source of joy. The joy is that no matter how far we may fall into sin, God never gives up on us. He is always offering us the grace to come back to him: first through the Sacrament of Baptism, and again and again through the Sacrament of Penance and Reconciliation. The Sacrament of Marriage gives us an image that both points to that joy and makes it happen:

Husbands, love your wives, as Christ loved the Church and gave himself up for her, that he might sanctify her, having cleansed her by the washing of water with the word, that he might present the Church to himself in splendor, without spot or wrinkle or any such thing, that she might be holy and without blemish. Even so husbands should love their wives as their own bodies. He who loves his wife loves himself. For no man ever hates his own flesh, but nourishes and cherishes it, as Christ does the

Church, because we are members of his body. "For this reason a man shall leave his father and mother and be joined to his wife, and the two shall become one flesh." This is a great mystery, and I mean in reference to Christ and the Church. (Eph 5:25–32)

By not only pointing to the love that Jesus has for the Church, but also making that love happen here on earth in the Christian family (CCC 1643), the Sacrament of Marriage sanctifies the world and prepares the Church for the fulfillment of its ultimate hope: the last day, on which she will be joined to Christ at his Second Coming, the Marriage Supper of the Lamb (Rev 19:1–10).

History and Theology

|| ASSIGNED READING
|| CCC 1601–1666

Impediments

Since the marriage of two baptized persons is a sacrament, and since God has given to his Church the power and the duty to safeguard the sacraments, the Church has the power and the duty to safeguard marriage. The Church safeguards marriage not to keep people away from it but to keep it safe, so that it will always continue to be an image of her relationship to Jesus (CCC 1647). It is similar with the Eucharist. We reserve the Eucharist in a tabernacle not to keep it away but to keep it safe, so that it will always continue to bring us the presence of Jesus and will not be defiled by sacrilegious profanation. If the Church permitted people whose relationships were not an image of her relationship to Jesus to marry, she would be contradicting the very purpose for which Jesus raised marriage to the dignity of a sacrament—something which the Church can never do. What is more, society would crumble if the Church did not safeguard marriage, because marriage is the basis of the family and the family is the building block of society (CCC 2207).

In order to keep marriage pointing to Christ's relationship with the Church, the Church has to have rules about who can get married and who can't, and to figure out who is married and who isn't. Those rules are centered around *impediments*. In general, an impediment is something that gets in the way of something else. Impediments to marriage get in the way of our getting married. There are two kinds of impediments to marriage: *prohibitory impediments*, which get in the way of our getting married in the way that we're supposed to, and *diriment impediments*, which get in the way of our getting married at all. Someone who has a prohibitory impediment *should not* get married; someone who has a diriment impediment *cannot* get married (CIC, Canon 1073).

Some diriment impediments to marriage are established directly by God because there is no way that someone subject to one of them can point to Christ's love for the Church in marriage (see CIC, Canon 1075, §1). No human authority, not even the pope, has any power to dispense from these. Others are established by the Church because there is some reason why, at a given place and time, someone subject to one of them would not be a good image of Christ's love for the Church (CIC, Canon 1075, §2). The Church can dispense from the impediments that are established by her if and when she feels that in a particular case someone could still point to Christ's love for the Church in marriage.

There are four basic diriment impediments to marriage established directly by God.

1. **Being unable to consummate the marriage** by performing the marital act. This can happen in two ways:
   - **Age:** Since marriage entails consent to engage in marital relations with one's spouse, a person who has not yet reached puberty cannot enter into marriage. In order to help marriage point to Christ's love for the Church better, the Church can establish higher minimum ages at one time or another. Presently the minimum ages are sixteen years of age for men and fourteen years of age for women (CIC, Canon 1083, §1).
   - **Impotence:** Again, since marriage entails consent to perform the marital act, a person must be able to perform vaginal inter-

course in order to enter into marriage. A person who, prior to marriage, is absolutely and perpetually incapable of engaging in that act cannot enter into marriage (CIC, Canon 1084, §1).

2. **Being directly related** by blood. This is called *consanguinity* when it applies to immediate family, and *affinity* when it applies to those to whom one is related to the fourth degree.

3. **Being already married** to someone else.
   - Since Christ took only one bride, the Church, a person who is already married cannot marry a second person (CIC, Canon 1085, §1).

4. **Being unable to consent to marriage** because of some problem with a person's deliberate intention. Christ freely took the Church for his bride and the Church freely responds to Christ's call. Anything that impedes the ability of a person to consent deliberately and freely to marriage makes it impossible to enter into marriage. This can happen either through a lack of *knowledge* or through a lack of *will*.
   - **Lack of Knowledge:**
     - If one lacks sufficient use of reason, discretion of judgment about marriage, or is otherwise mentally incapable of being married (CIC, Canon 1095).
     - If one is not aware "that marriage is a permanent partnership between a man and a woman ordered to the procreation of offspring by means of some sexual cooperation" (CIC, Canon 1096, §1).
     - If one marries the wrong person, or is mistaken about some quality "directly and principally intended" about them (CIC, Canon 1097).
     - If one is maliciously deceived about the other person deliberately so as to conceal something that would disturb the marital partnership (CIC, Canon 1098).
   - **Lack of Will:**
     - A man cannot marry a woman he abducts (CIC, Canon 1089), nor can anyone get married when forced to do so (CIC, Canon 1103). Christ did not kidnap the Church.

- A marriage cannot be based on some future condition (CIC, Canon 1102). Christ did not have a prenuptial agreement with the Church.

- Merely saying the words does not make two people married. Although the Church presumes that they mean what they say (CIC, Canon 1101, §1), it is possible to lie when they say the words by "a positive act of the will exclud[ing] marriage itself, some essential element of marriage, or some essential property of marriage" (CIC, Canon 1101, §2). Christ always means what he says, and when he took the Church for his bride, he meant it.

There are also six diriment impediments established by the Church. Since the Church has established these impediments, the Church can dispense from them if and when she sees fit.

1. **Marrying an unbaptized person if you are baptized** (CIC, Canon 1086). Since it is the Sacrament of Baptism that makes people members of the Church, only marriages between two baptized people point fully to the relationship between Christ and the Church.

2. **Having Holy Orders** (CIC, Canon 1087). Having Holy Orders binds a man to Christ directly; in the Latin Rite it also entails a vow of celibacy. Consequently, it is not appropriate for a man in Holy Orders also to bind himself to another human person.

3. **Having taken "a public perpetual vow of chastity in a religious institute"** (CIC, Canon 1088). Similar to the case of Holy Orders, a public, perpetual vow of chastity binds a person to Christ directly, although in a non-sacramental way. Consequently it is not appropriate for those who have taken such a vow to bind themselves to another human person.

4. **Murdering one's own spouse or murdering another person's spouse in order to marry that person** (CIC, Canon 1090). Christ does not destroy the Church to take another bride.

5. **Marrying someone in the direct line of ascent or descent of someone with whom you have previously cohabitated outside**

of marriage. This avoids grave scandal, which distracts from Christ and causes people to stumble in their relationship with him.

6. **Marrying outside the Church.** All Catholics who marry are obliged to get married according to the liturgy for marriage established by the Church, in front of "the local ordinary, pastor, or a priest or deacon delegated by either of them, who assist, and before two witnesses" (CIC, Canon 1108, §1). This protects the celebration of the Sacrament of Marriage from any alteration or denigration; since marriage points to the relationship between Christ and his Church, and since Christ only has one Church, it is fitting that marriage should take place visibly within that Church.

That probably seems like a lot of rules, but there is a purpose to all of them. Each of the situations described in some way prevents marriage from being an image of Christ's love for the Church: the rules given directly by God keep marriage as an image of Christ's love for the Church; the rules given by God's Church prevent marriage from appearing any other way here and now. The first group of rules are based upon the Church's knowledge of the truth about God, about humanity, and about marriage. The second group are based on two thousand years of experience in helping marriage to continue to point to Christ's relationship to the Church. Together, they help safeguard marriage so that we can continue to revere it, and so that by revering marriage we can revere Christ and his Church to whom marriage points.

Annulments and Convalidation

Whenever it turns out that two people held a wedding ceremony but one or both of them is thought to have been impeded by one of the diriment impediments mentioned above, either of the spouses or a special Church official called the "promoter of justice" can initiate proceedings for a Declaration of Nullity, or "annulment" as it is commonly called (CIC, Canon 1674). If either or both of them really were subject to a diriment impediment at the time, then although they had a wedding ceremony, they did not actually contract a marriage. We say in that case that their marriage was "invalid." That is a very serious situation. It means that two people who have been living together and thought they were married were not actually married. It is not a situation to be taken lightly.

The Church reveres marriage because the Church reveres the relationship she has with Christ, to which marriage points. For that reason the Church never wants to declare marriages invalid. When we put people on trial, we assume that they are innocent until proven guilty; when the Church puts marriages on trial, she assumes that they are valid until proven invalid by a complete, just, and fair judicial process (CIC, Canons 1060; 1085, §2). Even when it looks like a marriage might be invalid, the Church still tries to find ways for the couple to stay together. She offers to the faithful the possibility of a "convalidation." Convalidation, which can be offered to couples after any diriment impediments are removed (CIC, Canon 1156, §1), is a second chance at marriage. It gives the couple, whose first attempt was invalid, an opportunity to renew their consent to enter marriage now that any obstacles to it have been taken away (CIC, Canon 1157).

If convalidation is not possible or if the couple is resolute in not choosing it, when the Church issues a Declaration of Nullity, it is not a form of "Catholic Divorce." A Catholic annulment does not dissolve an already existing marriage; it declares that there never was a marriage in the first place (CCC 1629).

Separation, Dissolution, Divorce, and Remarriage

|| ASSIGNED READING
|| 1 Corinthians 7:10–16

If two baptized people have gotten validly married and have "performed between themselves in a human fashion a conjugal act which is suitable in itself for the procreation of offspring, to which marriage is ordered by its nature and by which the spouses become one flesh" (CIC, Canon 1061, §1), then their marriage "can be dissolved by no human power and by no cause, except death" (CIC, Canon 1141), because their marriage points to the permanent love that Christ has for his Church. That having been said, while marriage includes a grave obligation to live together with one's spouse, it is possible that there may arise grave circumstances that require the temporary or permanent separation of spouses from one another (CIC, Canon 1151). Legitimate reasons for separation include adultery (CIC, Canon 1152) and grave mental or physical danger (CIC, Canon 1153). Such separation is not to be undertaken lightly.

Except in cases of immediate danger, since the Church always wants to revere marriage, the law of the Church stipulates that separation must also be granted by an ecclesiastical court (CIC, Canon 1692, §1). Separation, moreover, is not necessarily permanent. The Church always wants to encourage forgiveness and reconciliation (CIC, Canon 1152, §1; 1155) and so requires that as soon as the need for separation ceases, the spouses resume living an ordinary married life together (CIC, Canon 1153, §2); they are, after all, still married (CCC 1649). In either case, whether or not ordinary married life can be resumed, the Church requires that the spouses provide for the needs of their children (CIC, Canon 1154).

When, on the other hand, a marriage is not between two baptized persons or it has not been consummated, it is possible in certain circumstances for the Church to dissolve it. When a marriage is not between two baptized persons, it can be dissolved *in favor of the faith*. This practice derives from St. Paul's instructions in 1 Corinthians 7:10–16.

Paul's language clearly supports marriage and supports married couples remaining together. Nevertheless, Paul envisages certain situations in which a married person wishes to convert to the Catholic faith, but his or her spouse refuses to live an ordinary married life with him or her after the conversion. In such situations, because of the actions of the unbelieving party, it would not be possible for a marriage to point to the relationship between Christ and the Church. The Church has received Paul's teaching in the form of the "Pauline Privilege," whereby the Church may grant the dissolution of a marriage between two unbaptized people *in favor of the faith* so that the person who wishes to convert may marry a Catholic (CIC, Canon 1146). Such dissolutions only occur after the unbelieving person is asked whether "he or she also wishes to receive Baptism" and whether, if not, "he or she at least wishes to cohabit peacefully with the baptized party without affront to the Creator" (CIC, Canon 1144).

Outside of the Pauline Privilege, the pope can also dissolve marriage in favor of the faith in which one of the two spouses is baptized. This is customarily called the "Petrine Privilege." Finally, the pope can dissolve a marriage between two baptized persons provided that the marriage has not yet been consummated (CIC, Canon 1142). This is not something that happens very often; the Church presumes that if married people have lived together for any length of time that consummation has occurred until it is proven otherwise (CIC, Canon 1061, §2).

Divorce does not exist in the Catholic Church, only outside of it. In the Church's law there are Declarations of Nullity, which establish that a marriage never existed; dissolutions of existing marriages by the Pauline or Petrine privileges; dissolutions of marriages between two baptized persons that have not yet been consummated; and the acknowledgement that since the Sacrament of Marriage points to the relationship between Christ and the Church and makes it happen between a man and a woman, a marriage that exists between two baptized persons and that has been consummated can never be dissolved by any person. The Church does, however, acknowledge the existence of civil divorce as a means of regulating the purely civil effects of marriage, over which the Church does not always have jurisdiction in civil law (CIC, Canon 1059).

Civil divorce does not in any way affect a person's marital status before God and his Church; only the Catholic Church has the authority from God to issue a Declaration of Nullity, a separation, or a dissolution. Nevertheless, in view of the practical consequences involved when the Church grants one of these three, the Church can permit Catholics to obtain a civil divorce where necessary to address the civil consequences of ecclesiastical actions. The appropriate time for a civil divorce is after the Church's judgment has been rendered about a marriage, unless permission is given sooner (CIC, Canon 1692, §§2–3).

Since divorce does not exist in the Catholic Church, obtaining a civil divorce does not have any effect on a person's ability to remarry. There are only three things that give a person the ability to remarry: the death of their lawful spouse, a Declaration of Nullity that establishes that they were never married to that spouse in the first place, or the dissolution of their marriage to that spouse according to the conditions stated above. Those who remarry after having only received a civil divorce are excluded from Holy Communion because they are leading a life that is not in accord with Christ's love for his Church, but directly opposed to it (CCC 1650).

QUESTIONS FOR REVIEW

1. How is marriage different from the other sacraments?
2. What was God's original plan for marriage?
3. How did marriage change after Jesus established the Church?
4. What does Jesus teach about divorce?
5. What are the four impediments to marriage established by God? What are the six impediments established by the Church?

QUESTIONS FOR DISCUSSION

1. Give an example of a healthy marriage you have witnessed. How could you see Jesus active in that relationship?
2. What do the various impediments to marriage teach us about the grace that God wants to give us in marriage? What makes marriage different from other relationships?

Chapter 2

LIVING THE SACRAMENT

|| ASSIGNED READING
|| CIC, Canons 1055–1165

Celebration

At the central moment of the Sacrament of Marriage, a baptized man and a baptized woman come before a representative of the Church—"the local ordinary, pastor, or a priest or deacon delegated by either of them"— as well as two witnesses (CIC, Canon 1108, §1), and exchange matrimonial consent: "An act of the will by which a man and a woman mutually give and accept each other through an irrevocable covenant in order to establish marriage" (CIC, Canon 1057, §2). That consent—expressed by the words, "I take you to be my wife" and, "I take you to be my husband" (CCC 1627)—makes the marriage (CCC 1626; CIC, Canon 1057, §1) and from it "arises a *bond* between the spouses which by its very nature is perpetual and exclusive; furthermore, in a Christian marriage the spouses are strengthened and, as it were, consecrated for the duties and the dignity of their state" (CCC 1638).

When a man and a woman exchange matrimonial consent, they themselves are the ministers of the sacrament, conferring it on one another through their mutual consent (CCC 1623, 1639). The presence of a priest or deacon is necessary not because the priest or deacon "marries" the couple but because the priest or deacon receives their mutual consent and blesses the marriage that they confer on one another in the name of the Church (CCC 1630).[1]

The presence of a priest or deacon also bears witness to the fact that marriage is not a private relationship. As the building block of society, marriage has a naturally communal character. As an image of Christ's relationship to the Church, marriage has a supernaturally ecclesial character. For this reason, marriage is ordinarily celebrated in the context of Mass. In this way, the covenant into which the man and the woman enter is sealed through the Eucharistic sacrifice by which the covenant between Christ and his Church is renewed (CCC 1621).

Effects of the Sacrament

The primary effect of the Sacrament of Marriage is the indissoluble bond it creates between the husband and the wife. Since that bond is a sacrament, it not only *points to* but also *makes present* between the spouses the love that Christ has for his Church; it "gives rise to a covenant guaranteed by God's fidelity" (CCC 1640). The grace arising from this bond makes perfect the love between the spouses so that their love may ever more attain to the likeness of Christ's love for the Church in its freedom, totality, faithfulness, and fruitfulness: *freedom* by the spouses' daily choice to love God, to whom their marriage points, and to love one another in the love that he gives them; perseverance in the *totality* of their commitment to God and to each other until death; exclusive and unique *faithfulness* to God and to each other; and *fruitfulness* in their relationship with God as well as through welcoming the children he gives them together.

The marital bond between a husband and a wife, which makes the love of Christ for his Church present, gathers the family with its children

---

[1] Note, however, that "in the tradition of the Eastern Churches, the priests (bishops or presbyters) are witnesses to the mutual consent given by the spouses [Cf. CCEO, can. 817], but for the validity of the sacrament their blessing is also necessary [Cf. CCEO, can. 828]" (CCC 1623). This means that the Church considers the lack of this blessing a diriment impediment to marriage in the Eastern Rites.

into a domestic church. This "domestic church," patterned after the Holy Family of Jesus, Mary, and Joseph, is an icon of the redemption of society, a window in the midst of a broken world into the happy life of union with God.

> It is here that the father of the family, the mother, children, and all members of the family exercise the priesthood of the baptized in a privileged way "by the reception of the sacraments, prayer and thanksgiving, the witness of a holy life, and self-denial and active charity" [LG 10]. Thus the home is the first school of Christian life and "a school for human enrichment" [GS 52 § 1]. Here one learns endurance and the joy of work, fraternal love, generous—even repeated—forgiveness, and above all divine worship in prayer and the offering of one's life. (CCC 1657)

The domestic church is a household's participation in the Church's sacramental life, which makes present the fulfillment of the Greatest Commandments. It is, moreover, the context in which the vast majority of people live out their relationship with God: a place where children, nurtured in the love that Christ has for them, are brought into the Church through the Sacrament of Baptism, formed in habits of humility and contrition through the Sacrament of Penance and Reconciliation, prepared for union with Jesus through the Sacrament of the Eucharist, readied for the pouring out of the Holy Spirit through the Sacrament of Confirmation, and sent out into the world as fully fledged members of human and Christian society to seek, find, and fulfill their own vocations.

Appropriating and Living This Sacrament

One of the most important duties of parents within the domestic church is to "encourage [their children] in the vocation which is proper to each child" (CCC 1656). For everyone, that is a vocation to love. "God who created man out of love also calls him to love [which is] the fundamental and innate vocation of every human being" (CCC 1604). It is a vocation that anticipates the eternity to which we are all called: the love of God and the love of neighbor at the Marriage Supper of the Lamb in heaven.

Some people are called to live in the reality of that love more directly here and now. These are the people whom God has called to forgo marriage on earth so as to anticipate the Marriage Supper of the Lamb. Those who answer this call choose virginity for the sake of the kingdom as priests, religious, and consecrated virgins. This is something that Jesus himself spoke about (Matt 19:10–12).

Consecrated life is not of itself a sacrament. But from the earliest days of the Church, it has been a part of the Church's life to which God has called members of his people. Importantly, though, there is no antagonism between consecrated life and marriage. Marriage points to and makes happen the very relationship that consecrated life anticipates.

Most people, however, are called to find a spouse, to point to and make present Christ's love for the Church with that spouse in the Sacrament of Marriage, and thereby to form a domestic church for the building up of human and ecclesial society. But how will we know to which form of marriage we are called—to the Sacrament of Marriage or to the consecrated life? Since God is the one who issues the call, we will only hear the call if we devote ourselves to prayer. The more faithfully we attune ourselves to hear his voice, the more faithfully we will attune ourselves to follow him wherever he would lead us.

If God does call us into the Sacrament of Marriage, there are several concrete steps we can take to appropriate and live this sacrament.

The first step is to prepare for it carefully: First, by prayerfully asking God to send us the spouse that would be best for our relationship with God. Second, by discerning God's call to marriage with that potential spouse in such a way as respects chastity and modesty—developing habits of friendship, joy, and mutual support, while avoiding vices that corrupt pre-married friendship like cohabitation and premarital intercourse. Third, by attending the marriage preparation offered to us by our parish and seeking out the wisdom of other faithfully married couples. Fourth, by receiving the Sacrament of Penance and Reconciliation so that we are prepared for as fruitful a participation in the Sacrament of Marriage as possible. Fifth, by being married in the Catholic Church so that our marriage, which points to the love that Christ has for his Church, may be sealed by the offering Christ gave to his Church in the Eucharist.

The second step we can take to appropriate and live the Sacrament of Marriage is to live it out faithfully: embracing God's call to the free, total, faithful, and fruitful love of our spouse when married and growing together with our spouse and our children in the sacramental life of the Church. This means, first of all, being open to new life in the context of our marriage. Second, it means raising our children in the Church. Third, it means setting an example in the Christian life for them so that the family becomes a school of the Lord's service.

The third way to prepare for marriage is to reflect on it prayerfully. Christ's love for the Church is something that we can never completely fathom. By prayerfully reflecting on the nature of marriage, which points to and makes that love present, we are drawn into a prayerful reflection on the whole of the Christian life: a free, total, faithful, and fruitful relationship with the Lord, awaiting the day when our relationship with God will be sealed for all eternity at the Marriage Supper of the Lamb.

SELECTED READING
John Paul II, General Audience of January 5, 1983, in *Man and Woman He Created Them: A Theology of the Body*, trans. Michael Waldstein (Boston: Pauline Books and Media, 2006), 103:1, 5–7

"I … TAKE YOU … AS MY WIFE"; "I … take you … as my husband." These words stand at the center of the liturgy of marriage as a sacrament of the Church. The engaged couple speak these words, inserting them in the following formula of consent: "I promise to be faithful to you always, in joy and in sorrow, in sickness and in health, and to love and honor you all the days of my life." With these words the engaged couple contract marriage, and at the same time they receive it as a sacrament of which both are the ministers. *Both, the man and the woman, administer the sacrament.* They do it before witnesses. The authorized witness is the priest, who at the same time blesses the marriage and presides over the whole liturgy of the sacrament. Further witnesses are, in a certain sense, all the participants in the wedding rite and in an "official" way some of them (usually two) who are specifically called witnesses. They must witness that the marriage is contracted before God and confirmed by the Church. In the normal course of events, sacramental marriage is a public act by which two persons, a man and a woman, become husband and wife, that is, the actual subject of the marriage vocation and life. . . .

The sign of the sacrament of marriage is constituted by the fact that the words spoken by the new spouses take up again the same "language of the body" as at the "beginning," and, at any rate, give it a concrete and unique expression. They give it an intentional expression on the level of intellect and will, of consciousness and the heart. The words, "I take you as my wife/as my husband" bear within themselves precisely that perennial and ever unique and unrepeatable "language of the body," and they place it at the same time in the context of the communion of the persons. "I promise to be faithful to you always, in joy and in sorrow, in sickness and in health, and to love you and honor you all the days of my life." In this way the perennial and ever new "language of the body" *is not only the "substratum," but in some sense also the constitutive content of the communion of the persons.* The persons—the man and the woman—become a reciprocal gift for each other. They become this gift in their masculinity and femininity while they discover the spousal meaning of the body and refer it reciprocally to themselves in an irreversible way: in the dimension of life as a whole.

Thus, the sacrament of Marriage as a sign allows one to understand the words of the new spouses, words that confer a new aspect on their life in the strictly personal (and interpersonal, *communio personarum*) dimension on the basis of the "language of the body." The administration of the sacrament consists in this, that at the moment of contracting marriage the man and the woman, with the suitable words and in rereading the perennial "language of the body," form a sign, an unrepeatable sign, which also has a future-oriented meaning, "all the days of my life," that is, until death. This is the visible and efficacious sign of the covenant with God in Christ, that is, of *grace, which is to become their portion in this sign as "their own gift"* (according to the expression of 1 Cor 7:7).

If one formulates the question in socio-juridical terms, one can say that between the new spouses a conjugal contract is stipulated that has a clearly determined content. One can say, in addition, that in consequence of this contract, they have become spouses in a socially recognized way, and that in this way the family as the fundamental social cell is constituted. This way of understanding it agrees obviously with the human reality of marriage, and, indeed, it is fundamental in the religious and religious-moral sense. Yet, from the point of view of the theology of the sacrament, *the key for understanding* marriage remains *the reality of the sign* with which marriage is constituted on the basis of man's covenant with God in Christ and in the Church: it is constituted in the supernatural order of the sacred bond requiring grace. In this order, marriage is a visible and efficacious sign. Having originated in the mystery of creation, it draws its new origin from the mystery of redemption in order to serve the "union of the sons of God in truth and in love" (*Gaudium et Spes,* 24:3). The liturgy of the sacrament of Marriage gives a form to that sign: directly, during the sacramental rite on the basis of the ensemble of its eloquent expressions; indirectly, throughout the whole of life. As spouses, the man and the woman bear this sign throughout the whole of their lives, and they remain as that sign until death.

QUESTIONS FOR REVIEW

1. What are the essential elements that must be present in a wedding ceremony for a marriage to take place?
2. Who are the ministers of the sacrament?
3. What is the primary effect of the Sacrament of Marriage?
4. What is the domestic church?
5. Does a change in one's emotions or feelings about one's spouse change the nature of the bond between them?

QUESTIONS FOR DISCUSSION

1. What challenges can make fidelity to one's marriage vows difficult? How can couples overcome those challenges?
2. What virtues do husbands and wives need to possess in order to be good spouses and remain faithful to one another? How can you start acquiring those virtues now?

Appendix

CHALLENGES

Can't a Person Go Directly to God without the Help of the Church or a Priest?

In order to approach God, we need his grace. Because of original sin, we are born without the original holiness and grace that Adam and Eve enjoyed before the Fall, but God has restored his grace to us in an even more wonderful way. He sent his Son, Jesus. As both God and man, Jesus reconciled us to God, overcoming our sins by offering his life on the Cross and conquering death by rising from the dead. Consequently, Jesus is the one mediator between God and man. All salvation and grace comes through him. To approach God, we must go through Jesus.

Before Jesus ascended into heaven, he told his disciples, "behold, I am with you always, to the close of the age" (Matt 28:20). While we cannot interact with Jesus face-to-face like the first disciples did, Jesus established the Church and the sacraments so that he could remain present and work among us not just in a theoretical or spiritual way, but concretely and even physically.

Jesus has united himself so closely to the Church that Scripture calls the Church the Body of Christ. The Church makes Christ present, bringing his love and mercy to the world by proclaiming the Gospel, caring for the poor, and, above all, continuing his work of sanctification and salvation by celebrating the sacraments. As we learned in Part I, the sacraments were established by Jesus as efficacious signs. They do not just point to something that God wants to do in us; they actually make it happen. This is because it is Jesus who works through them. When a priest baptizes someone, consecrates the Eucharist, or absolves someone's sins, he speaks the words of Jesus, and because Jesus is God, his words cause what they signify.

It is true that we can always pray to God on our own, and that personal prayer and private study of the Scriptures are important parts growing closer to God. Likewise, as we learned when we studied "Baptism of Desire" God can manifest his grace outside of the sacraments and even to people who (to all human appearances) are outside of the Church. However, the Church is the Body of Christ, and the sacraments are the work of Christ. They were established by Jesus to continue his presence and his work in a visible way on earth. In them, God comes to us. Thus, there is truly no more direct way to encounter God than through the Church and in the sacraments.

Can't God Forgive Us Directly When We Are Sorry for Sin?

The answer to the previous question applies to this question too. We cannot reconcile ourselves to God on our own. Rather, he takes the initiative and reconciles himself to us through Christ. Through Christ, we obtain forgiveness of sins. As we learned, Jesus carried out a ministry of forgiveness of sins on earth, and he gave the Apostles the authority to continue this ministry after he ascended to heaven and sent the Holy Spirit. The Church carries out this ministry of forgiveness especially through the sacraments of Baptism and Penance. These are the normal ways that God has established through Christ to forgive our sins.

It's true that God can forgive sins outside the normal sacramental way. For instance, he forgives the sins of those who are saved through the "Baptism of Desire." After Baptism he forgives our venial sins when we have perfect contrition. However, if we commit a mortal sin after Baptism, we need to seek forgiveness in the Sacrament of Penance.

As we learned in Part III, there are reasons Confession is ordinarily necessary for the forgiveness of mortal sins. Jesus handed on the ministry of forgiveness of sins to the Church and gave the authority to bind and loose sins to the Apostles and their successors, the bishops and priests. Your sins and your salvation are not just between you and God. God reconciles us to himself by making us members of the Body of Christ, the Church, so you need to be reconciled not just to God but to the Church, and the priest in Confession acts as the representative of the Church, receiving you back so that you can return to Holy Communion.

Confessing your sins is ordinarily necessary for this reconciliation, because to exercise the power to forgive sins and to assign an appropriate penance, the priest must know what your sins are and see that you are sorry for them. Moreover, confessing our sins is good for us and necessary for overcoming our sins and growing in holiness. It forces us to take responsibility for our sins and humble ourselves before God so that we are opened to his healing grace. Moreover, it often brings us a great sense of relief, and when we make a good Confession, the sacrament gives us assurance that we are truly forgiven. We have Jesus' word, spoken through the priest, and Jesus' word is effective.

Aren't the Sacraments Just Celebrations to Mark Significant Moments in Our Life?

Each sacrament gives a special grace, and often the grace of a particular sacrament does correspond to a significant event in our life. For instance, if we are baptized as a child, we receive supernatural life around the time we receive natural life. If we are confirmed as an adolescent, we approach spiritual adulthood about the time we approach natural adulthood. If we are married, we join in a natural partnership that has been elevated to the dignity of a sacrament.

However, these sacraments are not mere cultural customs by which we mark our lives. Rather, they are signs given to the Church by Jesus, by which God marks our lives with his grace. They are personal encounters with Christ, in which he gives us grace to save us and assist us in the particular circumstances of our lives. The life of grace presupposes and perfects the life of nature, so we often receive a sacrament at a time when our natural development makes us most ready or most in need of the grace of a particular sacrament, but this isn't necessarily always the case. For instance, someone who is raised in a non-Christian home but comes to believe in Christ later in his life is baptized when he is already an adult. This doesn't necessarily correspond to any significant natural development in his life, but the grace of the sacrament is still real: he receives the same new life in Baptism that an infant receives.

Is There Any Difference between Receiving Holy Communion in a Catholic Church and Going to Communion in a Protestant Worship Service?

The power to consecrate the Eucharist was given by Jesus to his Apostles. They passed this power on to their successors, the bishops (and the priests who assist them), by the laying on of hands in the Sacrament of Holy Orders. Only a man who has been ordained to the second degree of Holy Orders (the "presbyterate" or "priesthood") has this power from Jesus. This power is necessary for the bread and wine to be transubstantiated into the Body and Blood of Christ. Without it, there is no Eucharist and no Eucharistic sacrifice.

Generally speaking, Protestant Christians do not believe in Apostolic Succession or the Sacrament of Holy Orders in the same way as Catholics. They have not preserved the Sacrament of Holy Orders in an unbroken line of succession going back to the Apostles. Since their ministers do not have Holy Orders, they are unable to truly consecrate the Eucharist—the bread and wine they use in their services remain bread and wine.

While God certainly may offer his grace to Protestant Christians who participate sincerely in these services, and they may experience closeness to Jesus and their fellow believers in them, Jesus' Body and Blood are not present sacramentally as they are in the validly consecrated Eucharist. And, in fact, most Protestant Christians do not believe in transubstantiation or that the Eucharist is a sacrifice, so they would agree that their communion services are not the same thing as a Catholic Mass.

Because of these differences, it is not possible for a Catholic to receive communion in a Protestant worship service. The Eucharist is the ultimate expression of the unity of the Church, and our participation in it is a public expression of complete union in faith with the Catholic Church and, more specifically, of our belief in the Real Presence of Jesus in the Eucharist. Consequently, it is not possible to share the Eucharist where this unity of faith does not exist. Catholics should not receive communion in a Protestant worship service, and non-Catholics cannot receive Communion at a Catholic Mass.

How Do We Know That Any of the Sacraments Really Work? For Example, if a Person Dies after Receiving the Sacrament of the Anointing of the Sick, Does That Mean It Did Not Work?

We know that the sacraments really work because Scripture and Tradition tell us that God's words work and that God has given to human ministers the power to speak his words in the seven sacraments. Thus, we know that the sacraments truly do give us the grace that they signify. However, this grace is not something that can be directly seen or felt or measured.

Sometimes people do experience dramatic effects from the sacraments in the form of powerful emotions or sudden deliverance from sinful habits or physical ailments. More often, though, it is only when we look back over our lives that we see how Christ has touched us and helped us through the sacraments, giving us the grace we needed at the time to persevere in difficulty or grow in virtue and holiness. We should approach the sacraments with an openness to whatever grace God wants to give us through them, but either way, we know by faith that when we receive the sacraments with the right dispositions the grace they give us is real, whether we feel it at the time or not.

This is true of all the sacraments, including the Anointing of the Sick. Recall that the Anointing of the Sick has several effects. First of all, it provides grace for bearing the suffering of illness and the temptations that come with it. This grace provides strength, peace, and courage, and it forgives venial sins and heals the soul of effects of sin; if the person is unable to confess, it can forgive mortal sin as well. Furthermore, the sacrament unites the sick person to the suffering of Christ so that his suffering participates in the saving work of Christ. The strength that comes from these graces sometimes does lead to physical healing, but their primary effect is spiritual and is always present, whether physical healing occurs or not. If they do not lead to physical healing, then they help prepare the person for death, giving him forgiveness, courage, and peace, so that he is ready and eager to meet the Lord. In either case, we know that the grace of the sacrament is real, and we trust that God will use it to bring about whatever is for the spiritual benefit of the person receiving it.